Java
Web Magic

Java
Web Magic

BY JOSEPH T. SINCLAIR AND LEE CALLISTER

Hayden
Books

Java Web Magic

Library of Congress Catalog Number: 96-78597
ISBN: 1-56830-341-6

Printed in the United States of America 1 2 3 4 5 6 7 8 9 0

Trademark Acknowledgments

The Java Web Magic Team

Associate Publisher
John Pierce

Publishing Manager
Laurie Petrycki

Managing Editor
Lisa Wilson

Marketing Manager
Stacey Oldham

Product Development Specialist
Steve Mulder

Technical Editor
Fred Bremmer

Production Editor
Michael Brumitt

Publishing Coordinator
Karen Flowers

Cover Designer
Aren Howell

Book Designer
Gary Adair

Manufacturing Coordinator
Brook Farling

Production Team Supervisors
Laurie Casey, Joe Millay

Production Team
Dan Caparo, Janelle Herber,
Christopher Morris, Pamela Woolf

About the Authors

Joseph T. Sinclair's expertise on text-based multimedia authoring predates the Web and HTML, and he first created digital multimedia products for fun and business in 1992. He is a former member of the Board of Directors of the North Bay Multimedia Association (NBMA) in the San Francisco Bay area and founded the NBMA's Internet Special Interest Group (SIG), one of the first Internet SIGs in the Bay Area. As education director of NBMA, he was instrumental in starting the College of Marin's comprehensive digital multimedia extension program curriculum in early 1994 and taught multimedia courses there. He built the first multimedia gourmet food Web site in 1994 and has built numerous Web sites since. Although not a programmer, Mr. Sinclair has used computers for business since 1981. His books, *Creating Cool Web Databases* (IDG) and *Intranets vs. Lotus Notes* (AP Pro), both books for nonprogrammers, are the definitive books in their respective categories of Web-database technology and groupware for business and education. A graduate of the University of Michigan, Mr. Sinclair has taught as an adjunct faculty member at San Jose State University and Golden Gate University.

Lee Callister is a writer, consultant, and educator, specializing in multimedia on the Internet. Executive producer at his own Web development company, Way Out West Productions, he is also Webmaster at `http://www.digiville.com` and is currently developing an Internet program at the Digiquest learning center in San Rafael, California. Mr. Callister was a founder of the North Bay Multimedia Association and served as president of the organization for over two years, during which he produced a successful monthly lecture series featuring top multimedia producers, artists, and philosophers. At the same time he also published and edited a monthly newsletter called the *Multimedia Reporter*. Mr. Callister was one of the planning partners for the Digital Village Project at the College of Marin where he has consulted on curriculum development and taught courses in multimedia. He organized and produced the Electronic Picnic at the Digital Village, the adult multimedia competition at the Marin County Fair, and the Mill Valley Film Festival's first Interactive Showcase. He is a former television and video producer who has won a number of awards for his work, including two Northern California Emmys.

Dedication

This book is dedicated to all those who will put Java to good use for aesthetic or practical purposes to enhance the Web as an interactive multimedia publishing medium. *Joseph T. Sinclair*

To the light in my life, Ms. Fran Zine. *Lee Callister*

Acknowledgments

This book was fun to write. As a nonprogrammer, it is always fun to be able to incorporate multimedia programming created by others into one's digital presentations or even create such programming using authoring software. Thanks to the people at Sun, Java makes the perfect vehicle for doing so on the Web. Thanks also to the people at Aimtech, Macromedia, Sausage, Riada, and a few other software companies, nonprogrammers can use Java authoring programs to create Java applets.

A special acknowledgment goes to Lee Callister, my coauthor, who in early 1994 was the first person I knew to foresee the immediate and fantastic potential of the Web for interactive multimedia publishing (about a year and a half before Bill Gates discovered the Web). The first time I ever heard the word "Mosaic," it was spoken by Lee, and by the spring of 1994 everyone in his orbit was well aware of the Web's accelerating emergence as a powerful new medium. My thanks also to Lee for his good work on this book. Thanks to Steve Mulder, our development editor at Hayden, who was helpful in providing some focus for our efforts which otherwise may have gone off in too many different directions. Thanks also to Carole McClendon, our agent, who was helpful as always. Special thanks goes to the pioneering programmers who created the applets presented in the book and gave us permission to use such applets.

Writing books is tough on family life, and I would like to express special appreciation to my spouse Lani and my daughter Brook for their support in the months it took to complete this project and to Germaine Hatcher, Lisa Ghafouri, Nancy Stevens, Tonny and Terri Eilerson, and Cookie Napala for their help to Lani and me in looking after Brook.

Joseph T. Sinclair

Joe Sinclair is a friend, an articulate, knowledgeable writer, and a very persistent guy who has been proposing we write a book together since I have known him. I'm glad we picked this one. Java is going to transform the Web and this has been a great opportunity to learn how nonprogrammers like me can use it to add fun and excitement to their Web sites. A special thanks to the friends who have allowed me to use their photographs, artwork, and ideas to make the book more interesting, including Will and Debi Durst, Luong Tam, Kate Reed, Terry Burkes, and Wes Middleton. Thanks to my parents for encouraging my curiosity early on and standing behind me through all my twists and turns. And to Zia, who brings me cookies and makes me laugh.

Lee Callister

Hayden Books

The staff of Hayden Books is committed to bringing you the best computer books. What our readers think of Hayden is important to our ability to serve our customers. If you have any comments, no matter how great or how small, we'd appreciate your taking the time to send us a note.

You can reach Hayden Books at the following:

Hayden Books
201 West 103rd Street
Indianapolis, IN 46290
(800) 428-5331 voice
(800) 448-3804 fax

Email addresses:

America Online: Hayden Bks
Internet: hayden@hayden.com

Visit the Hayden Books Web site at http://www.hayden.com ∎

Table of Contents

Graphics & Buttons

Animation & Special Effects

Multimedia & Interactivity

Utilities

The Magic of Java

Java! The word is exciting and mysterious, conjuring up images of steamy jungles and hot rich coffee. It's an apt name for the computer language that is transforming the Web.

Now you can add the flash and functionality of Java to your Web site and you don't need to be a programmer to do it. This book strips away the mystery and shows you how to add clocks, calculators, charts, advertising banners, scrolling images, dancing text, buttons that trigger slide shows, animation, and sound. It's as simple as pasting an applet into your Web page and making a few changes in the applet's HTML parameters.

The possibilities are endless. Programmers all over the world are creating useful new applets that you can adapt to your needs and add to your Web site. No matter what you want to do, there's probably an applet or an easy-to-use Java authoring program already available to help you do it. For example, the "AppletAce: Banners" applet scrolls a text message across a background graphic.

No doubt, you already have found the Web to be a terrific text-based multimedia publishing system. It's not difficult to use HTML (HyperText Markup Language) and it is even easier with an HTML editor such as BBEdit or HTML Assistant Pro, or an authoring program such as Netscape Navigator Gold or Claris HomePage. You can do a lot on the Web without being a programmer. In fact, being a programmer isn't much of an advantage for authoring with HTML, a creative touch is more important.

Nevertheless, the Web as we know it has limitations. HTML is not well suited for page layout, moving images, or sophisticated programming. One way to overcome these limitations is to provide additional functionality in the form of embedded programs.

Java Web Magic

Macromedia's Shockwave, Apple's QuickTime, VRML, and Java programs embedded in an HTML document can open animated "movies" with streaming audio, 3-D virtual worlds with chat capabilities, vector graphics, video, and a truckload of new capabilities from converting dollars into pesos to delivering updated financial information from a database. As the Web matures into a prime publishing medium, this kind of integrated programming is becoming increasingly important. Many new technologies are enriching the Web, but the programming capability with the most promise is Java.

Can you as a nonprogrammer really use Java? Well, you're probably not going to program a word processor in Java to compete with Corel's new Java WordPerfect, but there's a surprising amount you can do now—and do easily. This book will help you get started. Over the next few years, your ability to use Java on the Web as a nonprogrammer will blossom, as useful Java applets flood the market and Java authoring programs get easier. As they say, "We ain't seen nuttin' yet." This book will help you use Java applets and show you how to create them using Java authoring programs. You will be able to brighten up your Web site the way you have seen others do on the Web.

The book will take you beyond today's Java practice of window dressing for Web sites into tomorrow's practice of functional Java programming, such as Cooper & Peters' online word processor.

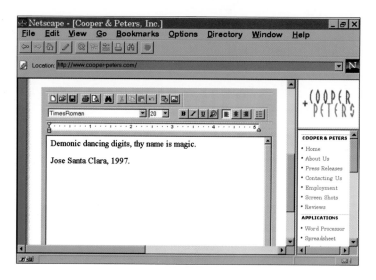

First, we'll review some basic principles and background information to help you better understand this programming language and why it's all the rage. If you're well-versed in Java basics and ready to start using applets, go ahead and jump right into the chapters on individual applets. If you want to better understand what makes Java different and how it works, read on.

Java Is Cross-Platform

Java is a cross-platform language—that is, it runs on any computer using any operating system as long as the Web browser is Java-enabled (for example, Netscape Navigator 2.0 or above, and Internet Explorer 3.0). The figures below show you the same applet (a slide show) from the same Web server running in both Windows and Mac browsers.

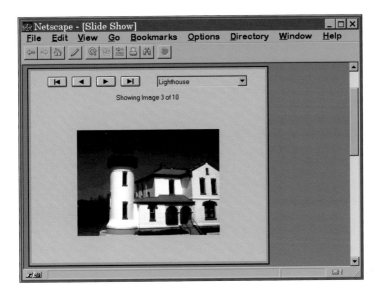

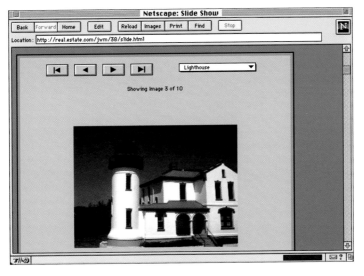

Unlike Java applets and programs, compiled programs written in older languages are specific to operating systems. Programs will run only in the operating systems for which they are written. Windows programs run on Windows 3.1, Windows 95, and Windows NT, but will not run on the Mac. Mac programs will not run on any version of Windows. Java programs run on computers that use Windows 95, Windows NT, Mac, Unix, and other operating systems. When you do your thing in Java, everyone can see it or use it.

Java Is Client-Side, Not Server-Side

There are two ways to provide programming functions that supplement HTML and HTTP (Hypertext Transfer Protocol).

- **Server Side:** CGI scripts are programs that conform to the Web Application Programming Interface (API), which is called the Common Gateway Interface (CGI). Such scripts can be written in any one of a variety of programming or scripting languages. CGI scripts run on the server computer that runs the Web server.

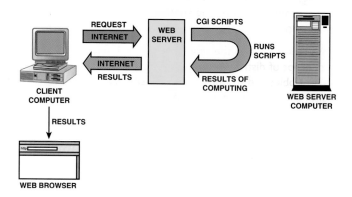

- **Client Side:** Java and JavaScript establish the infrastructure for distributed programs that are downloaded automatically from the Web server. They run on the *user's computer* rather than in the Web site computer, but are seen or used only with a Web client (browser).

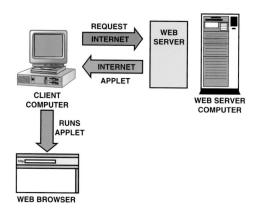

4

You can imagine that CGI scripts eat up a lot of a server computer's computing resources, particularly during times of heavy traffic. After all, a server provides network services for many clients; that means slowdowns. In addition, when many clients use a server for all their computing power, an inherently slower computing and network system results. Thus, a distributed programming system that invokes the power of client computers to run a portion of the programming used by Web site visitors is potentially faster, more efficient, and more powerful for all.

Java Is Object-Oriented

Java is an objected-oriented programming language. This means that each function programmed in Java is not just lines of programming code, but a self-contained programming module that includes two things that normal programming code does not have: its own data and the capability to communicate directly with other objects. For instance, a word processor might include 200 objects, but you do not need all of them at once. Perhaps the most you will ever use at one time is 15. If a server distributes objects to you over a network, it only needs to deliver to you the objects you need to get the current job done—a sort of "just-in-time delivery" of computing capability to suit the job at hand. The objects communicate with one another in your computer to provide you with a useful programming package.

This aspect of Java is well beyond the scope of this book, but it is appropriate for you to understand the concept of distributing objects over the network. A Java applet is an object, or a group of objects, distributed to a Web site visitor. The Web server sends the applet to the visitor's Web browser, where the visitor's computer runs the applet.

Java Is a Hybrid

There are two types of programming languages:

- **Interpreted:** These programming languages translate the human language into the machine language that computers understand, but they do it on the fly (in other words, while the program runs). The computer must translate the language at the same time it runs the program. As a result, interpreted languages run more slowly than compiled languages. All scripting languages (such as Perl and JavaScript) are interpreted.

- **Compiled:** These languages (such as C and C++) are translated into machine language *before* you use them and are compiled. When the computer runs a compiled program, it does not need to translate the human language into machine language. That has already been done by the compiler. As a result, compiled languages run faster than interpreted languages, perhaps as much as 10 times faster in some cases.

A program written in a specific language must be compiled separately for each operating system. Because each operating system is different, in order to be a cross-platform language (as an Internet-distributed language must be), Java must be an interpreted language. What can be done, if anything, to make Java run faster than a typical interpreted language? The Java developers at Sun Microsystems fashioned a unique solution. You compile Java for a *virtual machine*. Instead of translating Java into machine language, the Java compiler translates Java into *byte code* for the virtual machine. Each Web browser for each operating system has its own Java virtual machine built in. If this sounds complicated or even incomprehensible, it is enough for you to understand that Java runs faster than other interpreted languages, but not as fast as a truly compiled language. It's a hybrid.

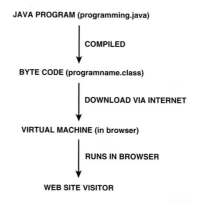

JAVA PROGRAM (programming.java)

↓ COMPILED

BYTE CODE (programname.class)

↓ DOWNLOAD VIA INTERNET

VIRTUAL MACHINE (in browser)

↓ RUNS IN BROWSER

WEB SITE VISITOR

Java programs have file names (such as programname.java prior to compiling). After compiling into byte code, the same program will have the name programname.class.

Using Java

There are three ways to use Java: JavaScript, Java applets, and Java applications.

JavaScript

JavaScript is a scripting language that is different from the Java programming language. It is strictly an interpreted language and is not compiled into byte code like Java. You place scripts (the actual programming code) in a Web page between the markup tags `<script></script>`. Because it is a scripting language, JavaScript does not offer the broad range of programming capabilities that a full-fledged programming language like Java does. JavaScript is not covered in this book.

Java Applets

These are Java applications programmed in the Java programming language and compiled. They are generally small, so as not to require long download times; but they do not need to be small. You place a reference to them in a Web page between the markup tags `<applet></applet>`. The applets are downloaded automatically into a Web browser. Marquee Lights, which puts moving lights around the border of a graphic image, is an example of an applet.

The HTML for Marquee Lights is simple. You can see it refers to the applet called MarqueeLights.class.

```
<applet code="MarqueeLights.class" width="220" height="324" align="middle">
<param name="image" value="dursts.jpg">
<param name="delay" value="150">
<param name="bulb" value="6">
<param name="border" value="6">
<param name="mode" value="RfbsFR">
<param name="gap" value="5">
<param name="url" value="/">
</applet>
```

The parameters (param) provide you with a way to easily change the applet for your own use and the "Getting Started" chapter takes you through changing the parameters for an applet step-by-step.

For large applets, it is a preferred practice to provide a button to start the program rather than have it download and start automatically. Corel uses a button to call the Java Office Suite.

After you click the button, the Office Suite programs are downloaded to your browser (which may take a few minutes).

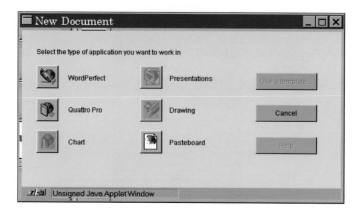

Java Applications

These are full-fledged computer programs written in the Java programming language. They exist like any other applications and *do not require a Web browser* to be used. They are beyond the scope of this book, but many programs already have been written in Java, and can be used like any other programs.

This book shows you how to install, use, or even author Java applets using authoring tools—not how to program applets. It's easy to do, but you should know some basic guidelines before you start. You'll learn about them in the next chapter. ■

Getting Started

You don't have to be an artist to add an image to your Web site, and you don't have to be a programmer to add an applet. But you do need to understand what components are necessary and how to add the requisite instructions to your HTML pages.

This chapter provides the programming specifics you need as a non-programmer to install, modify, and use Java applets. It's as simple as `<applet></applet>`, the HTML markup tags you use to install an applet in a Web page. To install a clock applet, just paste this `applet` statement into an HTML page.

```
<applet code="Clock2.class" width="112" height="25">
<param name="FontFamily" value="Helvetica">
<param name="FontSize" value="24">
<param name="FontWeight" value="bold">
<param name="DateFmt" value="%I:%M:%S">
<param name="BGCol" value="e60000">
<param name="FGCol" value="dcc800">
</applet>
```

The first line identifies the Java program or class file for this applet. The basic form is `code="programname.class"`. The `.class` extension shows that the source code was compiled using the Java compiler, as explained in the previous chapter.

```
code="Clock2.class"
```

The `code` attribute assumes that the class file is in the same directory (folder) as the Web page document itself. If you place the class file in another directory, you also need to use the `codebase` attribute, which specifies the path to the class file. This is in addition to—not instead of—the `code` attribute.

```
codebase="../otherdir"
```

You also can use the URL of a class file located on another server at another Web site.

```
codebase="http://www.otherserver.com/otherdirectory"
```

TIP Some applets require multiple class files (provided by the developer) to be present for the applet to work, but the linking between the files is automatic. Your `applet` markup will reference only one program file. However, you must make sure that you upload all the class files required by the applet to the proper directory on your Web site.

You find the applet's dimensions in pixels next.

```
width="112" height="25"
```

Your monitor's screen size is measured in pixels. Keep in mind that not everyone uses the same size screen, nor sees your image as you do. The three most common screen sizes are 640×480 pixels, an old standard still used by many people, especially Macintosh owners; 800×600 pixels, which is more common today with PC users with reasonably up-to-date computer equipment, and 1024×768 pixels for larger monitors. Most newer monitors display more than one size at different resolutions, so many people will decide for themselves what resolution they will use based on personal preferences as well as screen size.

640 x 480

It's safer to make your applets fit into the lowest common denominator, 640×480. After you consider the border of the Web browser window and provide an attractive margin of blank space around the Web presentation, you have about 550 pixels to use for width. Because most browsers include pull-down menus, tool buttons, and a URL window at the top of the window, more space is lost in the height dimension. So, about 320 pixels is the most you can use if you want the presentation to be completely visible to someone using a 640×480 screen. These estimates assume that people use their Web browsers set at full screen.

The applet `width`/`height` dimension statement will claim exactly that area for the applet. HTML will no longer control that area for setting background colors, fonts, and other visual elements. Such display elements must be set by the applet itself. If the applet does not load properly or some other malfunction occurs, the area set by the `width`/`height` dimension statement will usually appear in gray.

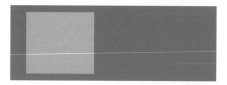

If you claim a space that is too large or too small for the applet, you are likely to have extra gray space around the applet or on two sides of it, or you might hide part of the applet.

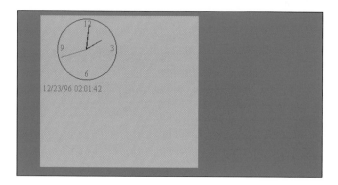

Be careful with the dimension statements. You may need to change the dimensions specified by the developers in some cases and experiment.

The same `alignment` attribute you use for HTML graphics also works with applets. Try `left`, `right`, `texttop`, `top`, `absmiddle`, `middle`, `baseline`, `bottom`, and `absbottom` to position the applet in the Web page. The `hspace` and `vspace` attributes enable you to create margins around the applet (measured in pixels) when it displays on the Web page. This often helps your HTML authoring, because you may not want text or other objects to butt up against the applet.

The `name` attribute enables you to distinguish between applets, if you have more than one included in a Web page. This is useful when you want the applets to communicate with each other, but it is not otherwise required and is beyond the scope of this book.

The parameter markup tag, `<param>`, gives you the capability to modify the applet's appearance or behavior. Each parameter has a `name` and `value` attribute specific to that applet. Change the value and you've changed the appearance or behavior.

Most applets start with parameters that specify visual elements. When you change the value you alter the appearance. Two common parameters are background color (`bgcolor`) and font color, `fgcolor` (foreground color), stated in a format similar to this example from the Clock2 `applet` statement:

```
<param name="BGCol" value="e60000">
<param name="FGCol" value="dcc800">
```

The color settings are usually expressed in hexadecimal numbers. Most people use RGB color numbers for doing digital artwork. The red background for Clock2 is 230,0,0 using RGB, and `E60000` using hexadecimal numbers. Most HTML editors and authoring programs now have functions that translate these numbers, but you may find it handier to use a utility RGB/hex converter program. A useful shareware translator program (for Mac and Windows) called HTML ColorPicker is available on the Web at `http://home-page.databank.com/vecdev/vector.html`. A useful book from which you can learn more about handling color in HTML documents is *Creating Killer Web Sites* by David Siegel.

 Use the same background color for the Web page and for the applet, and it will appear seamless. It doesn't work as well with tiled background images, where the seams sometimes show around the applet.

What are the other `applet` parameters you are likely to find between the `applet` tags? They can be anything the developer of the applet decides to provide you. For instance, Clock2 provides three easy-to-understand parameters for typesetting:

11

```
<param name="FontFamily" value="Helvetica">
<param name="FontSize" value="24">
<param name="FontWeight" value="bold">
```

The statement specifies Helvetica 24-point bold type. Be aware that in specifying font characteristics you are providing them for the user's computer. The user must have the fonts you specify or the specification will not produce the effect you are attempting to engineer. Although it is limiting, it's best to stick with Times Roman, Helvetica (Arial), and Courier, which the PC and Mac both use.

Many applets have special parameters related to their function. The Clock2 applet provides a parameter for determining how the applet expresses the time and date.

```
<param name="DateFmt" value="%I:%M:%S">
```

The characters %I, %M, and %S are some of many characters you can use to set the time/date format in Clock2. In fact, the developer of this applet implemented a mini-system with 23-character combinations—including the above three—that you can use to set the format. Another clock applet developer may not provide you the capability to set time/date formatting, or may use a completely different parameter setting system.

 The good news is that you can set a wide variety of time/date formats for Clock2 using the author's parameter statement without additional programming. The bad news is that it's like programming your VCR. This is typical of `applet` parameters.

Finally, you should know that Web browsers that don't support Java ignore the `<applet></applet>` tags, and they don't publish the information between them that is part of the parameter markups (`param`). The applet, of course, does not run. However, the `applet` statement publishes text and images between the `applet` tags that are not in parameter statements. In the following statement, browsers that are not Java-enabled publish the text and graphic in bold.

```
<applet code="Clock2.class" width="112" height="25">
<param name="FontFamily" value="Helvetica">
<param name="FontSize" value="24">
<param name="FontWeight" value="bold">
<param name="DateFmt" value="%I:%M:%S">
<param name="BGCol" value="e60000">
<param name="FGCol" value="dcc800">
If you don't have a Java-enabled browser, you will not be able to see or
use this clock.
<img src="sorry.gif">
</applet>
```

Keep in mind that you do not have to publish any text or any graphics for non-Java enabled browsers, but with an appropriately placed graphic (and no text), those with non-Java enabled browsers may not realize that they've missed anything.

Compiling Code

When was the last time you compiled something? If the answer is never, don't feel alone. Now is your big opportunity to compile some code, and it's easy to do. Everyone is doing it. On the Mac you simply drag-and-drop the Java file icon you want compiled to the compiler program icon.

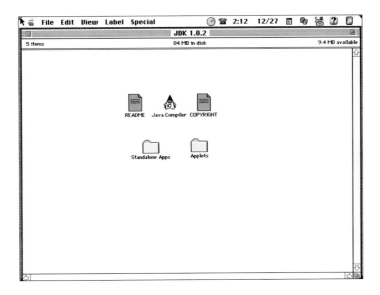

For Windows, you may need to use the DOS command line interface, unless you can find a compiler for Windows that works like the Mac. Doing it with DOS is an inconvenience, but it's easy.

Essentially, an uncompiled Java program is just a text file with multiple lines of programming code. For Java, such files have the extension .java and may be read in any plain-text viewer or in the plain-text mode in a word processor. But a file like programname.java is not ready to run. You must first compile it by using a Java compiler, which you can download free from the SunSoft Web site (http://www.sunsoft.com). It's in the Java Software Development Kit (Java SDK). Other software companies sell competent Java compilers, usually as part of a developer's tool software package. The Sun Java compiler for the PC is javac.exe, which you use on the command line together with programname.java in the DOS window of Windows 95 or Windows NT:

```
C:\>javac programname.java
```

A successful compilation on the PC simply returns you to the DOS prompt without fanfare. On the Mac, the new class file appears next to the java file, and the compiler moves into idle mode. In both cases the resulting file is a Java program ready to run: programname.class.

If the program is defective, the Java compiler will not finish the compiling process, and you will get an error message.

 Because you may have to recompile certain Java programs over and over again as you experiment with modifications (for example, the Smart Table spreadsheet developer covered in a later chapter), keep the compiler window open and ready to go. Some authoring systems (Smart Table, for example) include the Sun DOS Java compiler and must be run in the DOS window.

Why do you need to be able to compile Java? For many useful applets, the developer provides only the *source code* (in other words, programname.java), and you must compile the file. Some source code files do not even have the proper name for compiling (for example, programname or programname.txt), and you must change the name to programname.java before compiling. It is important to note here that you cannot otherwise change the name of the class or Java files. Java assumes that the name of the file coincides with the name of the class declared inside the Java file. If you change the name, the applet will not run.

Why do some developers supply source code and not compiled files? They do it for the convenience of those who desire to modify an applet for their own purposes. Modifying code is beyond the scope of this book, but programmers can save themselves time and effort by starting with someone else's code in some situations.

Tips for Using Applets

The previous two sections gave you a good start on how to incorporate applets into your Web pages. This section contains additional ideas and tips.

Working with Audio Files

Audio files must be in the 8 kHz .au format developed by Sun, a limitation that makes quality sound work more difficult. AIFF and WAV files use a higher sampling rate, which results in higher-quality sound but larger files. There are programs that convert other formats to .au files, but none that do it well as of this writing. Keep in mind that an applet downloads the sound files along with the applet. Audio files tend to be large, leading to long download times, so be careful that you do not bloat your applet beyond practical use.

```
   File  Edit  Control  Recording           2:19  12/27
                        Untitled1
 New York        12           B I U
 Normal
  0      1       2       3       4       5       6       7       8

        q

              SoundMachine Progress

              Atmos00.au

              8.0 kHz      00:00:02
```

Working with Graphic Files

Acceptable graphic formats are GIFs (.gif) and JPEGs (.jpg). Most applets recognize both. GIFs provide about 2:1 compression automatically. JPEGs, with a superior compression scheme, provide up to 10:1 compression with little loss in quality. Most image manipulation programs now include a built-in JPEG converter.

Remember to make all graphic files as small as possible to reduce download times. One way to keep them small is to limit the colors you use. GIFs are limited already to 256 colors (8-bit color). Operating systems and browsers typically reserve about 40 of those colors for themselves, so the number of colors available for a graphic is typically only about 216. With an efficient design you can probably get by with far fewer colors.

Often, JPEG compression produces a smaller file than a comparable GIF, and is normally better for photographs and large graphics. JPEGs are capable of displaying over 16 million colors (24-bit color) but will typically include only a few thousand colors in any one graphic. Although JPEG compression is lossy (loses picture quality), it starts out as a high-resolution image. Generally, you will find even a so-called low-quality JPEG is acceptable for Web use. For examples with different settings, see http://www.killer-sites.com.

Only GIFs index colors. Indexing one color to become transparent upon display gives you images that blend into the page rather than looking like they were patched onto it. You cannot do this with JPEGs.

It appears that JPEGs behave better and display better with Java. For almost all applets, JPEGs seem to be interchangeable with GIFs. Thus, you should consider using JPEGs wherever possible, unless they are considerably larger files than comparable GIFs.

Dealing with System Colors

Some applets use the operating system colors to determine the colors of certain visual elements in the applet's display (for example, the calculator keys on the personal calculator applet). Remember you have no control over the computer system colors of visitors to your Web site. Therefore, those visual elements displayed on a visitor's computer by the applet might be any color. Take this into consideration when determining how you will use the applet.

Keeping Notes

Keep notes on the dimensions and color numbers (both RGB and hexadecimal) for all your graphics (including backgrounds) as you work—that is, keep a pencil handy. It will save you a lot of time and energy.

File/Color	Size	Color [or GIF Index RGB]	Hex
ford.jpg	203 x 169		
house.gif	438 x 34	1192,192,192	C0C0C0
applet	379 x 153		
page background		166,230,166	A6E6A6
applet background		131,202,131	83CA83

Specifying Fonts

Although your use of fonts depends on what's installed in a visitor's operating system, you can get around this restriction by using your own fonts to make headings, and then turning them into GIFs with an image manipulation program. Reduce the color density to 4-bits (16 colors) so that the GIF compresses to a smaller file size than a normal GIF image. And make sure the text is anti-aliased, so you don't end up with "jaggies."

Printing

When you print a Web page that contains an applet, the page shows the applet area as a blank area regardless of what is displayed by the applet. Only an applet that is programmed to do so will print its contents. If an applet does print its contents, it prints them separately from the Web page.

Using Animation

Sophisticated animation like a Disney cartoon is beyond the capability of most computer users, but there many kinds of basic animation you can do with some help from Java. Add movement to your page with images and text that wipe or scroll up, down, or across the screen over multi-layered backgrounds. Liven up things with text that dances or zooms out toward the viewer. Add some flash to objects on your page with color cycling. All are simple forms of animation that you can use with applets in this book. Other programs let you assemble and play a series of images and control them with a mouse click. Egor lets you create a simple animation by drawing a path for an object across a background, and then outputting and compiling the code for you.

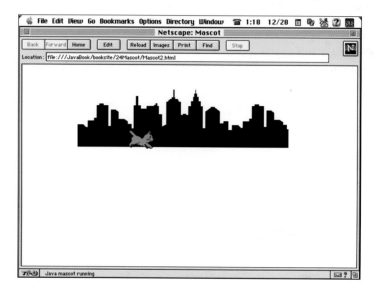

Testing Multimedia Performance

Asking your computer to handle more than one type of media at the same time can make extraordinary demands on a computer and its peripheral components. Some computers have more computing power than others. Some components have more power than others. Some combinations have more power than others. You should assume that your multimedia applets will run differently on your visitors' computer systems than on your own. Test the applets on as many systems as possible to see how well they perform.

Don't Duplicate

Don't duplicate HTML programming with Java just for the sake of using Java. What's the point unless you want to reduce the load on the Web server computer? Use Java for programming functions that are not available in HTML. For example, if you only want a simple animated graphic without audio, you can use an animated GIF without Java.

Staying Cross-Platform

It is important to note that there undoubtedly will be attempts by major software companies from time to time to create their own versions of Java that run only on their operating systems in power-play attempts to monopolize the market for themselves.

Using any version of Java that is not *pure*, however, will not work for a substantial portion of Web users. This is not a happy prospect and something to keep in mind when you choose applets to run at your Web site.

Displaying on TV

In 1997 the TV-Web wars will heat up with WebTV, ViewCall America, NetChannel, and others providing TV-centric Internet service for those who buy set-top boxes from Mitsubishi, Philips, RCA, Sony, and others. Because the set tops display the Web on a TV rather than a computer monitor, you should be aware of how you can maximize your use of Web pages and of Java applets when displaying on TVs. Information on doing so should become available from the TV Internet Service Providers in the spring of 1997.

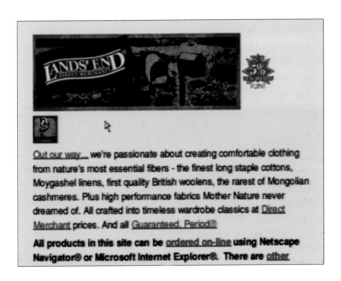

Spelling Case-Sensitive

Be sure in all your expressions of Java-related files and references that you pay close attention to upper/lowercase. Although HTML markup tags are not case-sensitive, assume that everything else is case-sensitive. This includes all information that you provide between the quotation marks in HTML tag attributes and all URLs. For instance, <applet> and <APPLET> are the same, but Clock2.class and clock2.class are not the same. The URLs http://www.bird.com and http://WWW.Bird.com are the same, but http://www.bird.com/robin and http://www.bird.com/Robin are different.

Using Zip and Cab Files

A number of computer files combined without compression into just one file is smaller than the sum of the separate files uncombined. Thus, Web browsers use Zip files and Cab (Microsoft) files to download Java classes more quickly. Don't mistake these files for their compressed cousins. These files are not compressed, but they do contain multiple files.

The zip file and path are indicated in the `archive` attribute which is part of the `<applet>` markup. The cab file and path are indicated in the `value` attribute which is part of a `<param>` markup named `CabBase`.

```
<applet codebase="hot/software" code="calc47" width="227" height="83"
archive="../classes/appletfiles.zip"><param name="CabBase"
value="../classes/appletfiles.cab"><applet>
```

Working with JBDC

Open Database Connectivity (ODBC) is a widely used standard Application Program Interface (API) for databases to communicate with other programs. If you have ODBC for connecting your database engine to a Web server in conjunction with CGI database applications, you may find Java Database Connectivity (JDBC), introduced in 1996, useful for Web-database systems using Java applets. This is a topic well beyond the scope of this book, but there are now many Java Web-database developments tools available, and some of them such as Mojo (`http://www.penumbrasoftware.com`) have been created for non-programmers with database experience to use.

Using the Most Recent Versions

If you like a particular applet from the CD-ROM, you might go to the appropriate Web site to get an updated version, as the applets are likely to improve. For instance, an applet that does not enable you to change the background color may enable you to do so in a future version.

Testing

Once you have installed an applet, test it on your own computer using your browser in *local host* mode (that is, access the Web page with Open File). If the applet doesn't work on your computer, it won't work online either. Remember, your Web browser must be Java-enabled—as all competitive browsers are today—in order to use Java applets.

Checking for Stability

Some Java applets are unstable or seem to require a huge amount of system resources. As a result, testing them on your own computer becomes tedious and can crash your system causing you to restart your browser or operating system often. Windows NT holds up reasonably well, but plan to reboot Windows 95 and the Mac fairly often, especially with multiple applets on the same page. Restarting from time to time to clear out the memory also seems to improve performance.

 Windows 95 seems to be an inherently unstable operating system. One way to give it more integrity is to run it with Windows NT 4.0 Workstation in the *dual boot* configuration provided by Windows NT. This doesn't make Windows 95 any more stable, but it does prevent those catastrophic crashes in Windows 95 that require you to go into the Safe Mode to rebuild the operating system. For this reason alone, it is worth it to run Windows NT (in dual

boot mode) to experiment with Java applets. Why not just use Windows NT? Unfortunately, some of your Windows 95 programs crucial to multimedia and Java authoring may not run in Windows NT.

This propensity for crashing operating systems is something to keep in mind when you load your Web pages with applets. You don't want to crash a visitor's browser or operating system. Even though there may be no harm done, it's an inconvenience that a visitor may not forget or forgive. On the other hand, some applets behave very well and don't seem to affect computing performance. Bad-actor applets presumably will be less of a problem in the future as the Java language matures and as programmers learn how to use Java.

Prices

This book and CD-ROM feature freeware, shareware, commercial software, and betaware. The authors made an effort to avoid high-priced software except in cases where comparable and acceptable inexpensive software was not available. Remember that shareware is trial software; after you've tried it and decide to use it, you are obligated to pay for it.

Finding Other Java Applets

Where can you find Java applets? Thousands of Java applets are now available on the Web. Some of the more massive collections are found at the following URLs:

- Gamelan: http://www.gamelan.com

- Jars: http://www.jars.com

- Java Centre: http://www.java.co.uk

- Sun JavaSoft: http://www.javasoft.com

Also, almost all of the Java applets in the book are on the book's CD-ROM, most complete with everything you need to adapt them to your own use.

21

Hiring a Programmer

Does it make sense to have a Java programmer develop a Java applet for you, or will it cost too much? This is a tough question to answer without discussing your project directly with a prospective programmer. For instance, programming mathematical functions is quite easy for a programmer. The logic is set and is not influenced by taste and other external criteria. All the programmer needs to do is make an easy translation (in other words, math to code), which will not cost much. On the other hand, making the resulting report from a mathematical computation look attractive on the screen or on paper may be a more difficult task for a programmer. It may require a lot of experimentation and tweaking depending on the complexity of the information to be expressed, and it may cost a considerable amount. Don't assume anything regarding the complexity or cost of a programming project until you discuss the project with a competent programmer. ■

Marquee Lights

This applet by Ken Shirriff (`http://www.sunlabs.com/~shirriff/java/marquee-lights.html`) is *tres* Hollywood. It turns an image into a movie marquee by surrounding it with a frame of flashing lights. "Nothing can be easier," say the reviewers. "All the work has been done for you." The truth is that the commands for the mode control settings, which determine the lighting combinations for the frame, are a bit murky. You can't go too wrong, however, because it's relatively easy to find a combination you like.

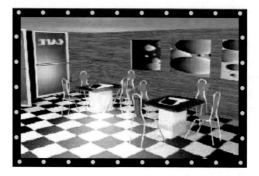

The applet uses HTML parameters to load a selected image and to set the configuration of lights around it. You can change the size and spacing of the light bulbs, the width of the border, and the speed. You also can choose between yellow and multi-colored bulbs. Using the mode setting, you program a series of events that play in succession before repeating itself.

If you want your image size to be accurate and not distorted, you need to enter its dimensions. Use an imaging or authoring program that tells you the width and height to specify in the applet markup tag. With another parameter, you can turn an image into a button as well.

Here are the parameters for the first example. You can see the flashing lights in action on the CD-ROM with this book.

```
<applet code="MarqueeLights.class" width="286" height="188"
<param name="image" value="cafe.jpg">
<param name="delay" value="150">
<param name="bulb" value="5">
<param name="border" value="10">
<param name="mode" value="f">
<param name="gap" value="5">
</applet>
```

22

Specify the name of the image you want surrounded by the marquee lights as the value in the first parameter. The delay value is the number of milliseconds you want the applet to pause between operations. A higher number is slower because it specifies a longer pause. The bulb value controls the size of the bulb, and the border value the width of the border. Both are in pixels. The gap determines the spacing between the bulbs.

For our first two examples we have set the delay value to 150 milliseconds, the bulb value (size) at 5, and the border value at 10. The gap between the buttons is set at 8. In each case this represents an average setting, and you can use it as a starting point. Experiment to find settings that fit your needs. There are no apparent limits, but it will quickly become obvious that some settings are too slow, fast, large, or small for what you want to do.

The mode setting is where you create a control string, or set of instructions to define the pattern you want the flashing lights to follow. The first image uses a simple f mode, which is a single stream of yellow lights moving continuously in one direction. It is possible to create a much longer string of instructions that includes a series of the following commands, as will be seen in the examples. Here are all the options:

- f: forward (clockwise), yellow lights.
- F: forward (clockwise), multicolored lights.
- r: reverse (counter-clockwise), yellow lights.
- R: reverse (counter-clockwise), multicolored lights.
- c: clear sequence (clockwise). The yellow lights all start out lit, and go out (are cleared) one by one.
- C: clear sequence, random order.
- s: set sequence (clockwise). The opposite of c. The yellow lights light up one at a time.
- S: set sequence, random order.
- n: no (all off), yellow lights.
- 1: one bulb only.
- +: additive. Two lights in opposite corners start running along the edges. When they reach the opposing corner, they stop moving and stay lit. A new set of bulbs then does the same thing, stopping beside the previous ones. This continues until the border is full of lights.

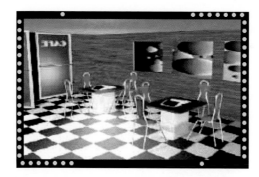

■ b: blinking. A string of lights flashes on and off on one edge, alternating with a longer string of lights around the rest of the border.

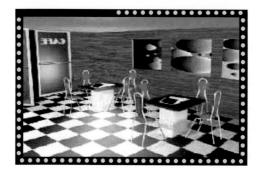

Experiment to see how changing the combinations affects the frame around your image. Remember that you can put combinations of these commands together into a single string to create a sequence of events.

Making the bulb size larger than the border results in marquee lights that intrude into the picture.

```
<param name="bulb" value="10">
<param name="border" value="5">
```

24

The `stride` parameter value describes a series of breaks that you can introduce into your light stream. For this image, the setting is 9 for this feature. A lower number gives you smaller breaks. Unlike gaps, which are breaks between individual bulbs, the stride breaks are between clusters of bulbs.

```
<param name="stride" value="9">
<param name="mode" value="RfF">
<param name="gap" value="12">
```

The relationship between the lights and the border in this example is the same as it was for the first image, but the multicolored element was turned on by changing the `mode` string to `RfF` (reverse multicolored stream, forward yellow stream, forward multicolored stream). Reducing the gap brings the individual light bulbs closer together.

```
<param name="gap" value="2">
```

25

Turning off the `stride` parameter again activates a steady stream of multicolored lights. Adding a new command b into the `mode` string introduces a new pattern of flashing yellow lights that you can see on the CD-ROM with this book.

```
<param name="bulb" value="6">
<param name="border" value="6">
<param name="mode" value="RfbFR">
<param name="gap" value="5">
```

The string `RfbFR` means reverse multicolored lights, forward yellow lights, b yellow "blink" pattern, forward multicolored, and reverse multicolored. The lights and border are both set at 6 and the gap at 5. The next image illustrates the "blink" part of the sequence.

You also can make an image into a button using this parameter to create a link:

```
<param name="url" value="http://www.anywhere.com/this.html">
```  ■

Water Reflection

Applet: lake.class

The Lake applet puts water with moving waves in front of a graphic (in other words, a digital photograph). This applet is the good work of David Griffiths of Leicester, United Kingdom (http://www.demon.co.uk/davidg/lake.htm).

The water shows a reflection of the graphic. This is quite an attractive applet, but its use is limited.

How does this cutie work? There's not much to it.

```
<applet code="lake.class"
width="237" height="300">
<param name="image"
value="wfall.jpg">
</applet>
```

Enter the width of the GIF or JPEG for the width attribute. You must, however, enter the height attribute of the graphic according to a formula. The formula is simple:

(height × 2)–10.

If the height of your graphic is 200 pixels, the correct entry for the height attribute is 390 or (200×2)–10.

All of the photographs in this chapter were cropped from larger photographs. You may need to experiment with cropping to get a bottom edge that provides attractive and realistic continuity for the final image.

To foster safety and also to avoid liability, most Web experts recommend that you warn your Web site visitors against swimming. ■

NO SWIMMING

Animated Mascot

Applet: mascot.class

Mascot, by Japanese programmer Masakazu Fujimiya (http://www.asahinet. or.jp/~FX6M-FJMY/), is an applet that you can use to create a playful little creature that follows your cursor and scampers over whatever background you choose, such as these images by Terry Burkes.

Installing the applet and changing its speed and background parameters is simple. The challenge is in preparing the images for the main character, which must use the names and postures specified by the applet's author. The cat on this page is from Fujimiya's Web site. You can replace it with any animal or alien creature built according to the specifications.

The default applet requires 11 separate image files, all of which must have the same width and height. They must be GIF files, and should have a transparent background. You should not anti-alias the images if you will be using them against a background image that is not a solid color.

The images needed include eight moving-image files, two stopped-image files, and one clicked-image file that match the following action postures and naming conventions:

- Two of the files portray upward movements. They must have the names imove1.gif and imove2.gif.

- Two of the files show movements to the right. They must have the names imove3.gif and imove4.gif.

- Two of the files portray downward movements. They must have the names imove5.gif and imove6.gif.

- Two of the files show movements to the left. They must have the names imove7.gif and imove8.gif.

- Two of the files will be used for stop positions. They must have the names istop1.gif and istop2.gif.

■ The image file that shows when the mouse is clicked must have the name iclick1.gif.

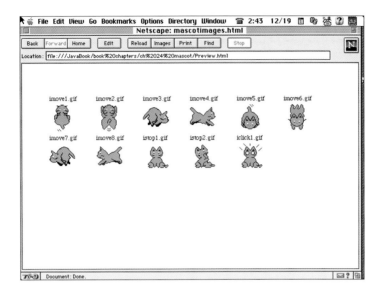

The code for the example shown earlier looks like this:

```
<applet code="mascot.class" width="450" height="120">
<param name="speed" value="4">
<param name="nimgs" value="2">
<param name="background_color" value="C0FFC0">
</applet>
```

Parameters you can add or change:

■ directory is an optional tag that lets you specify a path to your images if they are in another directory. The default is the same directory as the applet.

■ speed controls the speed of the mascot's movements. The default is 4.

■ nimgs lets you change the number of stop position image files. It must be an even number. The default is 2.

■ background_color establishes the background color value, which takes a six-character hex value. The default is light gray.

■ background_image enables you to designate an image file name for the background, which must be a GIF or JPEG file.

Mr. Fujimiya inserted a link to his own site in the lower-left-hand corner of the applet. If you want to remove it, you will have to change the Java file and then recompile it. He would like to know about any pages created in this way so that he can link to them. You can let him know via email at GEA03266@niftyserve.or.jp. ■

31

Animation

Applet: Animate.class

Animate by Cameron Gregory (http://www.bloke.com/java/Animate/) is a clever little applet that uses Java to create a simple looping animation from a series of still images (much like a GIF animation).

The basic configuration for this applet looks like this:

```
<applet code="Animate.class" width="75"
height="50">
<param name="img" value="anim-bloke-
small.gif">
<param name="onclick" value="default">
</applet>
```

Like any animated sequence the applet requires a sequence of images created in a paint or graphics program by someone with at least minimal art skills. What's different about this program is the way that it implements the animation. You must first combine all your images into one single image, laying them side-by-side like a comic strip panel. You also must set the width correctly. All the frames must be exactly the same width if you want the animation to run smoothly. Set the dimensions to the width of a single frame and it plays all the frames in sequence. The file Animate.class must be in the same directory as the HTML page.

The artwork for this animation was created by artist David Tompkins (http://www-cs-students.stanford.edu/~tompkins/). The GIF includes 75 separate images, which makes it run very smoothly. (Only eight of them can fit on the page at one time at this resolution.)

Another difference between these Java animations and regular GIF animations is the capability to stop and start the animation with a mouse click and control the timing by changing the parameters from the HTML document. You also can change the delay between frames and adjust the looping. As with a GIF animation, you also have the capability to turn the animation into a button by linking it to a URL.

It is not necessary to have so many images. The following animation, with artwork from Digiville.com (http://www.digiville.com) by Terry Burkes, uses only two images.

Here's what the configuration for this applet looks like. Note the extended delay after the first frame. Adjusting the delay dramatically changes the effect.

```
<applet code="Animate.class" width="120"
height="207">
<param name="img" value="downer.gif">
<param name="pause" value="2000">
<param name="loop" value="1">
<param name="onclick" value="default">
</applet>
```

With `loop` set at 1, this animation is set to play once and then stop. The onclick value determines what happens when a visitor clicks the mouse. Here it is set to default, which is looping. When a visitor clicks the mouse, the animation again loops the number of times specified in the `loop` parameter. The other option for onclick is the specified URL you want to link to from the image. When that is the specified value a mouse click takes you to the new location. Keep in mind that unless you do want to link to a new URL, you must specify default. If you just omit the parameter, the applet attempts to find a URL even though none is designated.

The complete list of parameters for the Animate applet includes:

- `img`: The URL of the GIF (for Netscape Navigator this must be on the same server).

- `pause`: Sets millisecond delay between frames (default 75).

- `fixedpaused`: Sets millisecond delay at end of animation (default 0).

- `randompause`: Sets random delay at end of animation. 0-`randompause` milliseconds (default 0).

- `loop`: Number of times to loop through; 0 means continuous looping (default 0).

- `onclick`: What happens when the user clicks the animation. Allowable values are default and URL. If you specify anything other than default, it treats the value as a URL and tries to load it. If the URL leads to an external helper application, the default action is also taken.

33

If you feel like experimenting with this applet, try using an abstract image and playing with the widths, which should create some unusual effects, or use multiples of the actual width to create a repeating animated header, footer, or horizontal rule. ■

Neon Sign

Applet: BlinkItem

Neon sign was created by Mattias Flodin, a Swedish student who made it for his own home page (`http://www2.bitstream.net/~gcagle/javax/`). It's an elegant but basic applet with no HTML parameters to modify other than the dimensions.

Here's the entire applet as it would appear in your HTML document.

```
<applet code="BlinkItem" width="494" height="243">
</applet>
```

The applet produces the neon effect by establishing a random blinking pattern that alternates between two images specified in the code. Its effectiveness depends on the skill of the artist creating the artwork. Here's the second image that alternates with the first.

To use this applet to create a neon effect like this, you need to create two images that are identical except for the colors of the "neon tubing" and any light spill patterns. These colors must be complementary, thereby suggesting the color and image patterns with the neon lights both on and off. Save and name them.

Because you can't modify any parameters, if you want to use this applet you will have to either use the same names and paths the author did or make changes within the Java file and then recompile it. Neither is difficult to do.

Flodin called his images Homepage1.gif and Homepage2.gif and put them in a folder called images adjoining his HTML document and class file. Your first option is to just give them the same names and create the same relationship to the HTML document and class file that he did. When the applet plays, it will find your images instead of his.

If you are feeling more adventurous this might be your chance to try your hand at compiling a Java file. As explained in "Getting Started," the Java file contains the original Java source code. Although opening and interpreting it is a daunting task for a non-programmer, this is a small, simple file and it's quite easy.

All you have to do is Open the BlinkItem.java source code file, replace the image references, and then compile it. The process is explained in "Getting Started." Just open the file in a text editor and look for the following reference:

```
// Load the two images in our 'animation'
imPic[0]=getImage(getCodeBase(), "images/Homepage1.gif");
imPic[1]=getImage(getCodeBase(), "images/Homepage2.gif");
```

Next replace the names of the images specified with the names of your own images, and place them in an adjoining folder called images (or else change the name and path to match what you have created).

Now save your changes, close the Java file, and compile it using the compiler in the Java Developers Kit (JDK) on the CD-ROM in the back of this book. The process is explained in the Getting Started section. On a Macintosh it's a simple drag-and-drop operation. Drag the file icon onto the compiler icon and after grinding away for a short while it spits out the class file (which in this instance is called BlinkItem). On Windows, you will be using the DOS command line interface which is less convenient but not difficult. The result is the same.

Now put the class file BlinkItem into the same folder as your HTML document and you are ready to go. The only other thing you need to remember to do is to change the size of the applet in the HTML document to match the size of your new images.

If your art skills are limited and you want some guidance in creating a simple neon sign, Hayden's *Photoshop Type Magic 1* book includes instructions for making a such a sign from a line of text.

Here is another sign, created for another Web page, that blinks:

You can use this applet to set up a random blinking relationship between any two images. In another example, a star on a logo blinks on and off when the images shown are substituted for the original images. ■

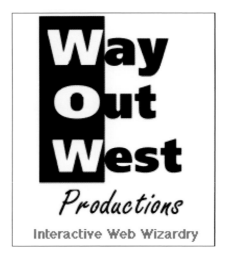

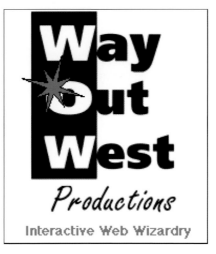

Dancing Text

Applet: CrazyText.class

This versatile applet by Patrick Taylor, from Template Software (http://www.nicom. com/~taylor/), is based on Daniel Wyszynski's NervousText applet, which was included as a demo in the Java Developers Kit. In both applets, a string of letters dances onscreen.

CrazyText spaces the characters much more evenly than Nervous Text, supports multiple lines of text, and adds double buffering to eliminate annoying flickers. It also incorporates a lot of new custom features with which you can play.

You control the selection of fonts, colors, and spacing. You choose the foreground and background colors, the appearance of a 3-D border and text shadow. You also can specify a URL to jump to when clicked, a message to display in the status area, a gradient fill for the background, and an image with which to tile the background.

Below are the two examples that appear on the front page of Taylor's Web site (and on the CD-ROM in the back of this book) with the key parameters. This demonstrates how two examples with complimentary features can be combined on one page to create a unique banner effect.

```
<applet code="CrazyText.class" width="310" height="65">
<param name="text" value="Add some spice!">
<param name="delay" value="100">
<param name="delta" value="5">
<param name="hgap" value="15">
<param name="clear" value="true">
<param name="cycle" value="char">
<param name="bgcolor" value="#c0c0c0">
<param name="bgImage" value="whitebg.gif">
<param name="borderSize" value="0">
<param name="borderOuter" value="0">
<param name="borderInner" value="3">
<param name="borderRaised" value="true">
<param name="shadowDepth" value="3">
<param name="url" value="none">
</applet>
```

- `delay` refers to the number of milliseconds between screen updates. The default setting is 100.

- `delta` controls the "craziness" factor, or maximum pixel offset. Its default is 5.

- `hgap` refers to the horizontal spacing (or kerning) between characters. In our first example it is set to 15. The default is 0.

- `clear` tells the applet to clear the background at each update.

- `cycle` tells the applet whether it should cycle colors for the individual characters (`char`), each line separately (`line`), the entire string of text (`whole`), or not at all (`none`).

- `bgcolor` defines the background color. Note that all color settings are determined by using the six-position hexadecimal system, which specifies a color's red, green, and blue components. (`#c0c0c0`, for example, is the hex setting for gray.) If you are not familiar with this system, you can find further details and examples at `http://www.infi.net/wwwimages/colorindex.html`. If you are a Macintosh user try the HTML Color Picker on the CD-ROM with this book. It's a useful tool that makes picking colors and converting them from RGB to hex numbers very easy.

You specify an image with which to tile the background with the `bgImage` value parameter.

In the second example, the `delay` is set to 500 (a much slower cycling rate) and the `delta` or craziness factor is eliminated by setting it to 0. Adding a second background color enables you to create a gradient fill, which is described in more detail later in this section.

```
<applet code="CrazyText.class" width="310" height="35">
<param name="text" value="Javatize your Web site">
<param name="delay" value="500">
<param name="delta" value="0">
<param name="hgap" value="0">
<param name="clear" value="false">
<param name="cycle" value="whole">
<param name="fgcolor" value="#000000">
<param name="bgcolor" value="#000000">
<param name="bgcolor2" value="#0000ff">
<param name="borderSize" value="0">
<param name="borderOuter" value="3">
<param name="borderInner" value="0">
<param name="borderRaised" value="true">
<param name="shadowDepth" value="1">
<param name="shadowColor" value="#ffffff">
<param name="fontName" value="Helvetica">
<param name="fontSize" value="18">
```

```
<param name="fontBold" value="false">
<param name="fontItalic" value="false">
<param name="url" value="none">
</applet>
```

Note the font characteristics in this version, which include:

- `fontName`. Java recognizes Helvetica, TimesRoman, Dialog, Courier, and Symbol.

- `fontSize` is the size of the font in points.

- `fontBold` makes it bold.

- `fontItalic` makes it italic.

There are also a series of parameters to define the look of the border:

- `borderSize` determines the thickness of the border in pixels.

- `borderOuter` determines the outer depth of the border.

- `borderInner` determines the inner depth of the border.

- `borderRaised` gives the border a raised look.

- `borderColor` enables you to specify a color in the form of a hex number.

You can also add a drop shadow to the text and link to a URL:

- `shadowDepth` adds a text shadow and determines its depth.

- `url` is a URL you want to link to.

Here are some more examples demonstrating some variations and additional parameters:

In this overlap `example` the delay value is increased to `250` and the `delta` or craziness value is minimized by reducing it to 3. This highlights the effect of overlapping the images, which is accomplished with this parameter:

```
<param name="clear" value="false">
```

You can see the results on the CD-ROM with this book. Setting the `clear` value to `false` means that when the image is updated (every 250 milliseconds) the previous image is *not* cleared. Instead, the new image is superimposed on top of the previous images.

A divider (or "pipe" character) between "Happy" and "Birthday" in the text value determines the line breaks in the next example, which has the hgap or horizontal character spacing set at 5 and is cycling the characters individually. This applet also illustrates a raised border, with a base value of 4, an outer perimeter value of 2, and an inner perimeter of 2.

```
<param name="text"
value="Happy¦Birthday">
<param name="hgap" value="5">
<param name="cycle" value="char">
<param name="borderSize" value="4">
<param name="borderOuter" value="2">
<param name="borderInner" value="2">
<param name="borderRaised" value="true">
```

Changing the cycle value to line results in all of the characters in each line cycling together. Setting the borderRaised value to false gives you a border that is recessed.

```
<param name="cycle" value="line">
<param name="borderRaised" value="false">
```

The color of the text for the Merry Christmas example does not change because the clear value is set to none. The red foreground color is picked up by the text and displayed against a light green background. A similar but slightly different red is selected for the border, which is set to 0, meaning it has no presence except for depth lines. Inner and outer perimeters for the border are both set at 2. A text shadow set at 2 is gray, the default color.

```
<param name="cycle" value="none">
<param name="fgcolor" value="#ff0000">
<param name="bgcolor" value="#a0ffa0">
<param name="borderColor" value="#c00000">
<param name="borderSize" value="0">
<param name="borderOuter" value="2">
<param name="borderInner" value="2">
<param name="shadowDepth" value="2">
```

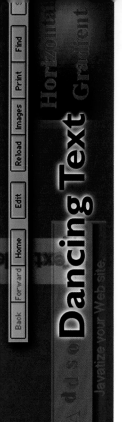

The next applet features a noncycling text string in front of a horizontal gradient. If the `bgcolor2` parameter is specified, a gradient fill appears on the background, starting with `bgcolor` and ending with `bgcolor2`. The `bgGradient` parameter specifies the direction of the gradient: `vertical` means top to bottom and `horizontal` means left to right. Be aware that gradients tend to look bad on 8-bit displays due to the limited color `palette`. Note that the specified font is bold and the shadow color has been set to `#a0ffa0`, which translates to a light green.

```
<param name="fgcolor" value="#ff0000">
<param name="bgcolor" value="#000000">
<param name="bgcolor2" value="#ffffff">
<param name="bgGradient" value="horizontal">
<param name="shadowDepth" value="1">
<param name="shadowColor" value="#a0ffa0">
<param name="fontBold" value="true">
```

Beware also of loading too many visual elements at once. This variation uses a vertical gradient plus a background image that renders the text in the frame as almost unreadable. Note that the transparency in the GIF file has been picked up is recognized by the applet.

```
<param name="fgcolor" value="#0000ff">
<param name="bgcolor" value="#ffffff">
<param name="bgcolor2" value="#000000">
<param name="bgGradient" value="vertical">
<param name="bgImage" value="smile.gif">  ■
```

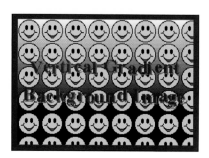

Scrolling Images

Applet: PicScroll.class, Scroller.class, sPic.class, StrExtract.class, ztl.class

Advertising banners are an obvious use for PicScroll, from Micro Nation Software (`http://www.flash.net/~hans/JavaCom/PicScroll/PicScroll.html`), which lets you scroll images across a designated background. With a variety of options for layering, positioning, and displaying images, the applet can add striking visual effects to any page.

For starters, you can designate a background image (or color) and then stack more images on top of it, specifying the size and position of the images in each layer.

You can then specify a series of other images to scroll across the backdrop you have created. Scrolling can be set to left, right, up, or down, in a window you define. You can scroll a single image through the window once, repeat it over and over, or play a series of images sequentially in order. Another option is to display a string of text in a message window at the bottom the applet.

In our first example from the Micro Nation Web site, a logo for a fictitious new search engine scrolls from right to left across a mountainous backdrop.

The length and complexity of the parameter set for the applet depends on how many of the features you want to use. The example shown uses three images once it is loaded: a static "logo" background and two scrolling graphic images that play in sequence and then repeat. Note that while PicScroll.class is the only class file you need to name, the applet uses five separate class files that must all be in the same directory as Picscroll. The others are Scroller.class, sPic.class, StrExtract.class. ztl.class. All five can be found on this book's CD-ROM.

```
<applet code="PicScroll.class" Java Applet" width="500" height="100">
<param name="foreColor" value="000000">
<param name="backColor" value="FFFFFF">
<param name="backTileImage" value="../pics/mnback.gif">
<param name="logoImage" value="../pics/newwhackyadvert.gif">
<param name="logoImagePos" value="0,0">

<param name="scrollDirection" value="left">
<param name="scrollSpeed" value="2">
<param name="scrollDelay" value="18">
<param name="scrollBoxPos" value="0,2">
<param name="scrollBoxSize" value="500,55">
<param name="scrollSpaceEvenly" value="yes">
<param name="scrollMakeCopies" value="yes">
<param name="pic1" value="../pics/altawho.gif">
<param name="pic1URL" value="../alta/altawho.html">
<param name="pic2" value="../pics/dot.gif">
<param name="pic2URL" value="../alta/mad.html">

<param name="mousyMessage" value="An Example Ad. Hope nobody gets mad.">
<param name="mousyMessFont" value="Helvetica,BoldItalic,14">
<param name="mousyMessColor" value="000000">
<param name="mousyMessSpeed" value="10">
<param name="clickToURL" value="PicScroll.html">
<param name="clickToURLinFrameName" value="_self">
</applet>
```

The foreColor and backColor settings are used only to determine the display that is seen while the applet is loading.

The optional backTileImage lets you establish a static image that is tiled behind everything else on the main window. The size of this window is determined by the dimensions set with the height and width attributes in the applet tag. Using an image the same size as the window eliminates tiling. Otherwise, the image will tile.

The setting logoImage establishes the next graphic viewers will see when the applet is running. In our example this is the mountain scene. Here it is the same size as the main window and covers the backTile image.

To position a logoImage that is smaller than the applet window, use the logoImagePos setting. This references the upper left corner of the logoImage from the applet's upper left corner. Here the setting is 0,0. The numbers refer to pixels. If you wanted the upper left corner of the logoImage to be positioned 10 pixels right and 20 pixels below the upper left corner of the main image, the values would be 10,20.

45

An optional `topImage` parameter lets you specify an additional image layer which sits on top of the other static images. This is the image layer which includes any scrolling images.

The next series of parameters are scroll controls, which control the images in the `topImage` layer. The images in this layer are the ones you want to scroll, which are specified as pic1, pic2, and so on. You can set `scrollDirection` to `left`, `right`, `up`, or `down`. The `scrollSpeed` setting determines the number of pixels the images will move for each animated frame. You can also set a `scrollDelay`, in milliseconds, between frames.

The `scrollBoxSize` setting defines the dimensions, in pixels, of a rectangular window that will contain the scrolling images. Note that a larger rectangle will slow down the animation, while too small a window will crop the scrolling images. Make the box large enough for the largest image.

You can establish the position of this box within the applet with `scrollBoxPos`, which like `logoImagePos` references the applet's upper left corner. Note that this `scrollBox` stays in a fixed position and does not move. It is only a window for the scrolling images.

Set `scrollSpaceEvenly` to `yes` to evenly space the centers of a series of scrolling images. A `no` value gives you images that are edge to edge. If you choose `yes` for `scrollMakeCopies`, the scrolling images will repeat themselves so that the scroll box always contains an image.

The next series of parameters is where you specify the names of the images you want to scroll. They are numbered pic1, pic2, pic3, and so on. You can also specify a linked URL for each image using pic1URL, pic2URL, and so on. Another option is a target frame for the link to open into. For our first picture the parameter would be pic1URLFrame.

There is also a series of parameters to set an optional message you can program to scroll across the bottom of the applet. Use `mousyMessage` to activate the string, and `mousyMessageFont` to determine the font name, style, and size.

The available Java fonts are Helvetica, TimesRoman, Courier, Dialog, and ZapfDingbats, and the recognized styles are Plain, Bold, Italic, and BoldItalic. The spelling and case of the letters is important, but you can use any size larger than zero. You can also set the text color (`mousyMessColor`) and scroll speed (`mousyMessSpeed`).

Finally, there are parameters to set a generic or default URL (which responds to a mouse click anywhere on the applet not otherwise specified as a linked image) and to target a frame. The value `self` loads it over the existing frame.

Another pseudo-ad from the Micro Nation Web site takes a whimsical approach to promoting a fast oil-change center, with scrolling images of a series of vehicles that includes tanks, helicopters, airplanes, and even a bee.

 We can change your oil, no matter what you drive!

Other than the name of the specified `logoImage`, and `scrollDirection`, which is up instead of `left`, this banner uses the same code as the last one until we come to the size of the scroll box and its position in the applet. The window this time is narrower and higher, and it is positioned at the right end of the applet.

```
<param name="scrollBoxPos" value="319,1">
<param name="scrollBoxSize" value="160,78">
<param name="scrollSpaceEvenly" value="no">
<param name="scrollMakeCopies" value="no">
```

The scrolling images are not evenly spaced this time, nor are individual images repeated. Instead the images scroll up through the frame in sequence. There are six separate image files in the scroll.

```
<param name="pic1" value="../pics/tank1.gif">
<param name="pic2" value="../pics/helicopter.gif">
<param name="pic3" value="../pics/glider.gif">
<param name="pic4" value="../pics/tank2.gif">
<param name="pic5" value="../pics/biplane.gif">
<param name="pic6" value="../pics/bug1.gif">
```

If you had everything, where would you keep it?

A final example, created just for fun, shows how you can use this applet to create a different look. A pair of red, painted lips scrolls across a woman's face and off the edge of the screen.

There are three layers of static images at work here, a backTileImage (a series of blue balls on a black background), a LogoImage (the woman's face), and a topImage (a black bar that partially covers the blue bars at the bottom of the applet).

The scrollBox containing the lips sits on top of the three static images. For each object except the TileImage, there is again a pos or position control that establishes a location based on the number of pixels the object is to the right and down from the top left corner. The first number is the amount of inset from the left margin. The second is the distance from the top.

With only one image programmed to scroll, setting the scrollMakeCopies control to no results in a single occurrence of the scroll instead of a loop.

```
<applet code="PicScroll.class" width="300" height="233">
<param name="backTileImage" value="blueball.jpg">
<param name="logoImage" value="ana.jpg">
<param name="logoImagePos" value="60,32">
<param name="topImage" value="black.gif">
<param name="topImagePos" value="0,212">

<param name="scrollDirection" value="right">
<param name="scrollBoxPos" value="158,121">
<param name="scrollBoxSize" value="125,107">
<param name="scrollMakeCopies" value="no">
<param name="pic1" value="lips.gif">
```

The red text at the bottom of the screen scrolls in from the right as a mousyMessage when triggered. The message is also linked to another page, and programmed to open it in the current window.

```
<param name="mousyMessage" value="If you had everything, where would you
keep it?">
<param name="mousyMessFont" value="Helvetica,Bold,12">
<param name="mousyMessColor" value="ff0000">
<param name="mousyMessSpeed" value="10">
<param name="clickToURL" value="link.htm">
<param name="clickToURLinFrameName" value="_self">
```

Working copies of the class files for PicScroll and a complete list of parameters are available at the Micro Nation Web site or on the CD-ROM in the back of this book. These are demo copies, which will work on your desktop but require a registration number to work on the Web. You can get one from the company for $45. ■

Twinkling Star

Applet: OliStar.class, sPic.class, StrExtract.class, ztl.class

OliStar, from MicroNation Software (`http://www.flash.net/~hans/JavaCom/OliStar/OliStar.html`), creates an eye-catching star effect you can use for a bullet, accent, or highlight.

Your star can be just about any size, with as many points as you want. The points can be tiny or reach out some distance from the star. The star also can shrink and grow, and can use any border color or fill color. It can have a static image on top of it or one underneath it and a colored background or image to blend in with the rest of the Web page. Images can be JPEG or GIF and the latter can include a transparent color.

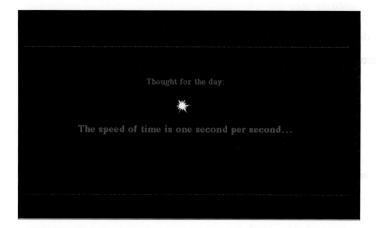

Here's the script for a simple accent point:

```
<applet code="OliStar.class" width="30" height="30">
<param name="foreColor" value="000000">
<param name="backColor" value="000000">
<param name="backTileImage" value="BigRedLeather.gif">
<param name="starFillColor" value="FFFFFF">
<param name="starBorderColor" value="E40A0A">
<param name="starCenter" value="15,15">
<param name="starPointRadius" value="15">
<param name="starUnpointRadius" value="6">
<param name="starPoints" value="12">
<param name="starDelay" value="30">
<param name="starShrinkAndGrow" value="yes">
<param name="clickToURL" value="OliStar.html">
<param name="clickToURLinFrameName" value="_self">
</applet>
```

OliStar uses some of the same class files and parameters as its cousin applet from the same company, PicScroll (see the previous chapter). Note that four separate class files are required: OliStar.class, sPic.class, StrExtract.class, and ztl.class, all of which must be in the same directory. Only OliStar.class must be referenced in the HTML document.

As with PicScroll, the foreColor and backColor settings determine the display that is seen while the applet loads, and the optional backTileImage enables you to establish a static image that is tiled behind everything else on the applet. Make the applet's background color the same as the background used for the entire page and your applet will blend seamlessly. You also can add additional layers of images, as you can with PicScroll. When using a backTileImage, you may find that testing and adjusting the size and location of your applet makes it fit more smoothly into the page.

A new set of parameters controls the image and behavior of your stars:

starBorderColor sets the color of the star's border, and starFillColor determines the interior color of the star. You can call the most common colors by name, or you can enter the hex code for the color you want.

The setting starCenter positions the star. Set values in pixels for the distances you want the star center to be right and down from the applet's upper-left corner. The setting 15,15 means 15 pixels to the right and 15 pixels down from the corner.

You can set the maximum radius of the star in pixels with starPointRadius, and the radius of the valleys between the star's points with starUnpointRadius. Use starPoints to establish how many points your star will have. (By the way, if starPoints is an odd number, the points won't be evenly distributed around the star. Two of the points will end up too close together.)

There is also starDelay, which sets the number of milliseconds between animated frames, and starShrinkAndGrow, which you should set to yes if you want the star to periodically shrink and grow. With this parameter set to yes the star will periodically shrink down to a point and then expand again. When the parameter is set to no the star will spin and the points will alternate lengths, but the star will not shrink down to a point.

51

Use the `clickToURL` setting to establish a link from the star to another URL. OliStar also allows you to target a specific frame where you want the new URL to appear, which you can name in the `clickToURLinFrameName` parameter. In our example the value self-loads the new URL over the existing frame.

If you want to use this applet to create a series of bullet points, make the applet smaller and repeat it several times.

The example below has a new `backTileImage`, a different color for `starBorder`, and new radius settings.

Notice that `starPointRadius` is reduced to 10 and `starUnpointRadius` to 3 and that the number of `starPoints` this time is 8.

```
<param name="starPointRadius" value="10">
<param name="starUnpointRadius" value="3">
<param name="starPoints" value="8">
```

Another interesting way to use OliStar is as a highlight for a logo or other image.

In this example, the applet and the star are both much bigger. There are new star colors and a new background image, and the radius has longer points. The star also is positioned where we want it on the logo image (by adjusting the `starCenter` parameter); the logo image is moved down and to the right (with the `logoImagePos`

control) to make room for the extended star points. Remember that the two numbers refer to the distance in pixels from the upper-left-hand corner of the applet. Here are the parameters that have changed:

```
<applet code="OliStar.class" width="205" height="240">
<param name="logoImage" value="wowLogo.gif">
<param name="logoImagePos" value="15,10">
<param name="starFillColor" value="E40A0A">
<param name="starBorderColor" value="000000">
<param name="starCenter" value="50,96">
<param name="starPointRadius" value="45">
<param name="starUnpointRadius" value="7">
```

At the bottom of the logo is a line of red text that scrolls in from the left when a mouse signal enters the applet space. This is another option also found on PicScroll. You can control the font as well as the text color and style, scroll speed, and links.

```
<param name="mousyMessage" value="Interactive Web Wizardry">
<param name="mousyMessFont" value="Helvetica,Bold,12">
<param name="mousyMessColor" value="E40A0A">
<param name="mousyMessSpeed" value="10">
<param name="clickToURL" value="http://www.digiville.com">
<param name="clickToURLinFrameName" value="_self">
```

Use mousyMessage to activate the string, and mousyMessFont to specify the font. To set the text color and scroll speed, use mousyMessColor and mousyMessSpeed, respectively. As with PicScroll, there are also parameters to set a generic URL (which responds to a mouse click anywhere on the applet other than on a designated button) and to target a frame.

Working copies of the class files for OliStar and a complete list of parameters are available at the MicroNation Web site or on the CD-ROM in the back of this book. These are demo copies that work on your desktop, but require a registration number to work on the Web. You can get one from the company for $25. ∎

Scrolling Text

Applets: FunScroll.class, FunScrollAbout.class, FunScrollAnimatedText.class, FunScrollColorSupport.class, FunScrollTextAttr.class

FunScroll, by Jan Andersson from Torpa Konsult AB in Jönköping, Sweden (`http://www.algonet.se/~jannea/FunScroll/FunScroll.html`), enables you to build a variety of text and image scroll effects into your page—with or without a surrounding frame.

FunScroll is more complicated than it appears on the surface, with many variables you can change. Five class files are required to run the applet, all of which must be installed in the same directory. FunScroll.class is the only one that needs to be referenced in your HTML document. You will find all the class files on the CD-ROM with this book, along with examples of text files that can be accessed by FunScroll, and complete lists of the parameters and tags that the applet supports. FunScroll is free for noncommercial use. If you want to use it commercially there is a $30 license fee.

```
<applet code="FunScroll.class" height="100" width="460">
<param name="line0" value="<25>Enjoy your garden now...<down> ">
<param name="line1" value="<40><up>You may have to move
tomorrow.<left>">
<param name="fgcolor" value="#0000FF">
<param name="bgcolor" value="#FFF5E2">
<param name="frameType" value="ShadowEtchedIn">
<param name="frameWidth" value="5">
<param name="frameMargin" value="10">
</applet>
```

Enjoy your garden now...

You may have to move tomorrow.

Message lines are where you specify the text you want to appear onscreen, and the effects and styles that you use to display it. You can incorporate up to 31 different message lines in this applet, identifying each one with the line<n> parameter (where <n> is a number from 0 to 30).

Add tags to a message line to specify the type of animation you want:

- <up> is a command to scroll up.
- <down> is a command to scroll down.
- <left> is a command to scroll left.

- `<right>` is a command to scroll right.

- `<explode>` makes characters explode.

- `<nn>` is a command to delay the animation `nn` frames.

In this example, message `line0` pops on the screen and after a delay of 25 units, it scrolls down off the screen. (The delay varies from computer to computer, so you should experiment.) Message `line1` scrolls up onto the screen, pauses, and then scrolls off the screen to the left. No text color was specified for either message line, so the applet uses the color specified for the foreground, which is blue. The name of this parameter is `fgcolor`.

There are also three parameters that are used to control the border given to this example, which are discussed in more detail below.

The tags for this applet are identified (by default) by the delimiters: <>. You also can change the delimiters to some other character (details below). This is useful when the information is displayed on a non-Java enabled browser that can become confused by the <> delimiters.

Many animation and style tags can be used to determine the direction of the scroll, the delay, and the text style. The following series of instructions are all for a single example that you can see on the CD-ROM with this book.

```
<applet code="FunScroll.class" height="100" width="460">
<param name="line0" value="<25>You are what you eat">
```

The first message line in this example (`line0`) has no animation tag, and pops on the screen where it remains for a 25-unit delay. Blue is the foreground color, which is also the default here.

> You are what you eat

The second message line (`line1`) uses the nervous style, and is assigned a color that translates as red.

> Help, I'm falling and I can't get up!

```
<param name="line1" value="<25>
<nervous><color=#FF0000> Help!
I've fallen and I can't get up!">
```

The third message line (`line2`) uses the sine-wave style.

> Life is full of little ups and downs...

```
<param name="line2" value="<25>
<sine-wave>Life is full of little
ups and downs...">
```

> **Wake up, and smell the toast!!**

There is a sequence of movements for the next line: scroll up, delay, and then scroll down. The delay is set at 15 units.

```
<param name="line3" value="<15><up>Wake up, and smell the
toast!!<down>">
```

> Today is the last day of your life so far.

This time use the name red instead of the hex notation. The action is similar to the last one, but another delay has been added before the downward scroll.

```
<param name="line4" value="<15><up><color=red>Today is the last day
of your life so far.<15><down>">
```

> **If the shoe fits - wear it. If it doesn't,**
> **maybe they have gloves in your size.**

New here is a line break, which is created by inserting the characters \n at the point where you want the break to take place. The text is centered by default.

```
<param name="line5" value="<up>If the shoe fits - wear it. If it
doesn't,\nmaybe they have gloves in your size.<up>">
```

> **Life is what happens to you**
> **while you are planning your next move.**

This time an align=left tag is added.

```
<param name="line6" value="<up>
<align=left>Life is what happens
to you\nwhile you are planning
your next move.<up>">
```

> **If your expectations are low enough,**
> **you might just get what you want.**

align=right works exactly the same.

```
<param name="line7" value="<up>
<align=right>If your expectations
are low enough, \nyou might just
get what you want. <up>">
```

The specified font for the applet is 20-point Helvetica, and the font style is bold. You also can choose italic. The default is normal.

```
<param name="font" value="Helvetica">
<param name="style" value="Bold">
<param name="size" value="20">
```

#0000FF is the hex number for blue—again the foreground color and default text color for this applet.

```
<param name="fgcolor" value="#0000FF">
<param name="bgcolor" value="#FFF5E2">
```

The frame around the applet is ShadowEtchedOut. The other choices are ShadowEtchedIn, ShadowIn, and ShadowOut. Try each one to see the effect. You also can set values for the frame width and margin, which establishes a margin between the frame and the applet.

```
<param name="frameType" value="ShadowEtchedOut">
<param name="frameWidth" value="5">
<param name="frameMargin" value="10">
</applet>
```

The next example uses the text style attributes engrave, emboss, and shadow. All of these attributes work best with larger fonts. The font used here is 32-point bold Times Roman.

Here the choice is shadow text.

```
<param name="line0" value="<20>
<down><shadow>This is shadow
text">
```

This is shadow text

And in this example the choice is engraved text. The engraving effect uses a darker shade of the background color.

```
<param name="line1" value="<20>
<down><engrave>This is engraved
text">
```

This is engraved text

Here is embossed text. The embossing is based on an outline that is a slightly darker shade than the background color.

```
<param name="line2" value="<20>
<down><emboss>This text is
embossed">
```

This text is embossed

And here the shadow and nervous effects are used together.

```
<param name="line3" value="<20><down><shadow><nervous>Cool! ...but also
slower..">
```

57

Cool! ...but also slower..

In this example we have also removed the border and changed the font from 20-point Helvetica to 32-point Times Roman.

You can make the text move faster (and less smoothly) by assigning dx, dy, and delay parameters. This example also uses a different frame border.

```
<applet code="FunScroll.class" height="100" width="400">
<param name="line0" value="<20><down>The text can move faster<up>">
<param name="line1" value="<left>In both directions">
<param name="line2" value="<left><sine-wave><20>A two-liner
with\nsine-wave...">
<param name="delay" value="50">
<param name="dx" value="3">
<param name="dy" value="2">
<param name="bgcolor" value="#FFF5E2">
<param name="frameWidth" value="4">
<param name="frameType" value="ShadowOut">
</applet>
```

The text can move faster

In both directior

Two-liner with
sine-wave...

The setting dx specifies the number of pixels to move horizontally for each animation sequence. The setting dy specifies the number of pixels to move vertically. The setting delay is a general delay that affects the entire applet, as opposed to a single line. It is measured in milliseconds, with a default of 100.

> Lines can also be split
> like this
> into a group of lines...

A tiled background image is added in this next example. It is displayed as soon as it loads. A different delimiter is used here to separate the tags. As you can see, you can define a new delimiter character using the `delim` parameter.

```
<param name="delim" value="#">
<param name="line0" value="#down#You can specify colors and background">
<param name="line1" value="#down#As well as Font">
<param name="bgImage" value="back.gif">
```

FunScroll gives you the capability to link a URL to any message line. To do so, add a `url` parameter line after the message line, with a number that corresponds to the message line. You also can specify a target window for the URL. `TARGET=_self` puts the newly loaded URL into the same window you have been using. `TARGET=_blank` opens a new browser window. Note the use of an alternate delimiter again.

```
<param name="delim" value="#">
<param name="line0" value="#20#Click to select one of the following
URL's">
<param name="line1" value="#down#30#FunScroll Main Page#down#">
<param name="url1" value="16FunScroll.html TARGET=_self">
<param name="line2" value="#down#30#Parameters#down#">
<param name="url2" value="params.html TARGET=_blank">
```

Click to select any of the following URL's

FunScroll Main Page

FunScroll applets also can read messages from a linked text file, in this case a file called text.data. You can call it anything you like.

Here is the data in the text file. Note that only the variables are listed, not the parameter tags.

```
<20>Text, initialized from file: text.data
<nervous><color=blue><15>Nervous (blue) text...
<sine-wave><color=#78DF95><left>Sine-wave (green) text...
<15><up>Scroll up, delay, and scroll down<down>
<15><up>Line with line-break\ncontinuing here.<down>
<15><up>Swedish chars: ≈ƒ÷Å‰ˆ
```

This is the parameter that appears on the HTML document to establish a link to the text file.

```
<param name="lineData" value="text.data">
```

If the link is to a nonexisting file, the user receives an error message.

Instructions for a link to another URL can be located in an external text file in the same directory, like this one which is called text2.data. You can give it any name you like. The target instructions load the information into a new browser page.

```
<applet code="FunScroll.class" height="100" width="400">
<param name="lineData" value="text2.data">
<param name="target" value="_blank">
```

You can generate message lines from CGI scripts, which are specified using the lineData parameter. To see the effect of using the applets with a CGI script, go to the applet author's site at
http://www.algonet.se/~jannea/FunScroll/FunScroll.html.

In this example the CGI script is a simple shell script designed to display the current time. The updateInterval parameter executes the CGI script at specified intervals. In this case 1 is specified. In other words, the applet reads from the CGI script once per animation frame.

```
<param name="lineData" value="http://www.algonet.se/htbin/cgiwrap/
~jannea/date.cgi">
<param name="updateInterval" value="1"> ■
```

> Thu Jan 23 19:43:08 MET 1997

Ripple Animation

Applet: ripple.class

The ripple graphic applet developed by David Griffiths, Leicester, United Kingdom (http://www.demon.co.uk/davidg/ripple.htm) provides the capability to create a color graphic with an internal wave animation. All you need to provide is one graphic. The applet does the rest. Look at the developer's blue graphic, which shows the text "the Ripple applet." It's a simple GIF. When combined with the Ripple applet, however, it waves.

The applet uses the following parameters expressed in HTML:

```
<applet code="ripple.class" width="190" height="190" >
<param name="image" value="ripple.gif">
<param name="period" value="25">
<param name="frames" value="12">
</applet>
```

See the GIF substitution, which includes the name of the artist Degas in a museum exhibit banner.

Substitute the name of your GIF file for ripple.gif and the dimensions of your GIF image. Remember to put your GIF in the same folder as the applet. You also can change the period and frame values. The period control sets the wave size. For a longer wave, use a higher number. The frames control sets the number of animation frames. It takes more frames to smooth out the action of a larger wave.

The dithering seen in the rippling image is unavoidable. A JPEG graphic file with more than 256 colors looks better than a GIF when it ripples, as you can see in the JPEG version of the Degas graphic.

An additional parameter

```
<param name="bordergap" value="on">
```

enables you to show the border of your JPEG or GIF as it shifts back and forth. This is distracting but can be useful for special effects.

The size of your graphic can vary. A wide graphic with a short height can produce a nice effect.

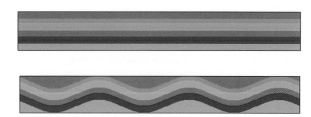

You should experiment with parameter settings for every GIF or JPEG that you use with the Ripple applet. If you do not set the parameters correctly, the graphic will not ripple smoothly. Make sure that the screen resolution of your graphic is 72 dpi during the development process for best results, because it will display in 72 dpi on a monitor as a GIF or JPEG.

You can produce a special effect by using a special JPEG. For instance, by putting a one-color border abound the JPEG, you can create a central art object that ripples. The Bolivian flag JPEG is a good example.

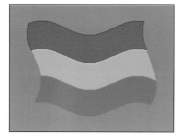

If you make the border the same color as the Web page, the graphic appears to ripple on the Web page. Making the border a transparent color in a GIF, however, does not work.

By intentionally setting improper parameters, you can get some bizarre but potentially attractive special effects. For example, set the period to 150 and the frames to 5 for a wild effect that is not adequately captured by a static graphic.

Stripes show off this applet well, but try some other graphics with it, such as patterns, textures, individual objects, and abstract art.

 Computers cannot handle many Ripple applets at once and your computer may crash if you use more than one in the same Web-surfing session. Keep this in mind when you incorporate them into your Web pages. ■

Slide Show

Slide Show

Applet: SlideShow.class, SlideCanvas.class, SlideImagePreparer.class, SlideImageRedrawer.class, NewButton.class

You can use this applet developed by Sean Hu and Randall Landaiche, KnowledgeSet of Mountain View, California, (`http://www.kset.com/cool/SlideShow/`) for any photographic or artistic presentations appropriate for your Web site such as photographs, works of art, maps, graphs, diagrams, line art, and other graphics.

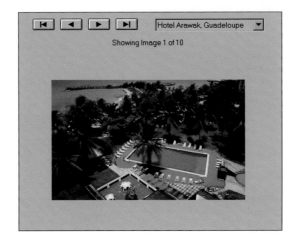

```
<applet code="SlideShow.class" width="500" height="400">
</applet>
```

The applet is functional with buttons for beginning of sequence, forward, backward, and end of sequence. The captions appear in a window that also acts as a pull-down menu from which to choose your slides.

The area for showing slides provides for flexibility in size, but cuts off slides larger than approximately 305×225 pixels. The Snapshot size (Base/4) of Kodak's Photo CD is 384×256 pixels and does not quite fit into the space provided. Therefore, they are cropped significantly unless reduced in size prior to showing. Photographs over approximately 20K seem to render the applet inoperable. The applet itself needs a little window dressing.

```
<img src="hbarblk.gif"><br>
<img src="smvbarblk.gif"><img src="hbar.gif" align="absbottom"><img
src="smvbarblk.gif"><br>
<img src="vbarblk.gif"><img src="vbar.gif"><applet code=SlideShow.class
width=500 height=400>
</applet><img src="vbar.gif"><img src="vbarblk.gif"><br>
<img src="smvbarblk.gif"><img src="hbar.gif" align="top"><img src=
"smvbarblk.gif"><br><img src="hbarblk.gif" align="top">
```

Use the following window trimmings:

- hbarblk.gif = 514×2 black

- smvbarblk.gif = 2×5 black

- hbar.gif = 510×5 rose

- vbarblk.gif = 2×400 black

- vbar.gif = 5×400 rose

Slide Show

The applet system provides an easy method of substituting your slides and captions for the ones that come with the applet. Just put them into a plain text file called images.txt in the following format:

```
"slides/68001.jpg"  "Hotel Arawak, Guadeloupe"
"slides/68008.jpg"  "Sunset, Guadeloupe"
"slides/68016.jpg"  "Budding flowers, Guadeloupe"
"slides/68044.jpg"  "Beach, Montego Bay"
"slides/68050.jpg"  "Windsails, Jamaica"
"slides/68053.jpg"  "St. Barthelemy"
"slides/68073.jpg"  "Before Sunset, Guadeloupe"
"slides/68074.jpg"  "Boats, Guadeloupe"
"slides/68089.jpg"  "Fishing boats, Martinique"
"slides/68095.jpg"  "Antique Map"
```

The photographs (or any images) go in a subdirectory (subfolder) named slides, off the directory that holds the applet files and the Web page. Remember that graphic files require extended download time.

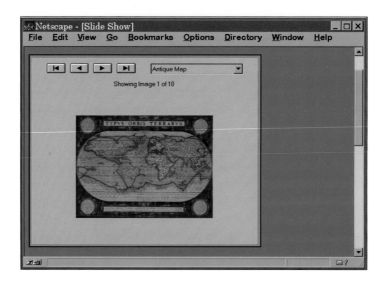

If you have not tried Kodak's **Photo CD**, take a roll of film in to your photo finisher today. You get back negatives, thumbnail prints, and each photograph digitized on a **CD-ROM** in five different sizes. This is a high-quality system—all for a cost of less than $30. ■

Rollover Button

Applet: HiBut.class

HiBut, the Highlight Button, is a simple but clever applet that enables you to specify up to four images and sounds that can be used sequentially with buttons or page adornments. Created by Casey Connor at the Center for Engineering Computing at Washington University (http://www.cec.wustl.edu/~casey/pages/hibut.html), this applet provides a quick, easy way to add mouse highlights and visual button clicks with accompanying sound, or to introduce some fun elements to your page.

You can give an applet up to four image URLs, which can be retrieved and used as the normal, highlighted, selected, and active button images. The normal image appears onscreen when the applet first appears. The highlighted image is activated by moving the mouse over the image; the selected image when you push down on the mouse; and the active image when you release the mouse, triggering a link. Applying the same logic, you can supply .au sound files to play in each position as you will see below.

Here is an example illustrating the four steps. To hear the sounds, play the applet on the CD-ROM in the back of this book.

```
<p><center>
<applet code="HiBut.class" width="104" height="48">
<param name="usebase" value="code">
<param name="normal" value="linen1.gif">
<param name="highlight" value="linen2.gif">
<param name="select" value="linen3.gif">
<param name="active" value="linen4.gif">
<param name="normalsound" value="none">
<param name="highlightsound" value="Atmos01.au">
<param name="selectsound" value="click.au">
<param name="activesound" value="Applause.au">
<param name="highlightsoundloop" value="yes">
<param name="URL" value="anyFolder/anyPage.html">
<param name="verbose" value="yes">
<param name="name" value="Linen">
</applet>
</center>
```

To create your own button, specify your image and sound URLs in the parameters and place them in the directory with the HTML document and HiBut.class file or create a path to them.

Keep in mind that Java currently supports only JPEGs and GIFs, and Sun's .au audio format. The .au files must be 8-bit sound, sampled at 8.012 kHz, with ulaw compression.

Converting sounds from other formats can be a challenge, sometimes requiring the use of more than one program. If you are downsampling from a higher rate, you will need to squeeze the dynamic range of the sound before converting it. Otherwise it will lose the highs and sound flat and hollow.

For the Macintosh there is a very versatile shareware program called SoundHack, which makes the process easier. Open your file in SoundHack, using either the Open or Open Any command, which even reads files without soundfile headers. In the latter case you will need to add header information prior to processing using the Change Header option under the Hack menu. An optional way to do this is to use a program such as SoundEdit 16 version 2 from Macromedia, which will easily convert just about any format to a 16-bit linear version of Sun's .au format (but won't downsample it to the requisite 8-bit, 8.012 kHz mode).

Next, downsample your sound file in SoundHack using Varispeed under the Hack menu. Set it to 8.012 kHz, and click Process.

A window will open with pop-up menus for file type and file format. Choose sun (.au) for the file type, and 8 Bit uLaw for the file format and then save your work. Once the processing is completed you can hit the spacebar to hear the new sound. Save it and you are ready to write it into your applet. (Another simple but useful audio player/conversion program for Mac users is SoundApp.)

71

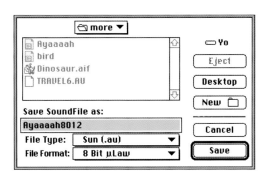

For the Windows platform there is a shareware program called GoldWave, which will convert a variety of audio files to Java-friendly .au files with a minimal loss of fidelity.

Note that in the example `normalsound` was left empty. HiBut is quite robust. You give it all or none of the parameters and it adapts. Even if you leave out one of the URLs, it still runs.

Any of the sounds assigned to a button can loop (play repeatedly) by adding a `soundloop` parameter like this.

```
<param name="highlightsoundloop" value="yes">
```

Another parameter, which is not shown in our examples, specifies whether or not nonlooping sounds stop in the middle when the applet is suspended (when the browser leaves the page, for example).

```
<param name="stoponleave" value="no">
```

The default value for the `stoponleave` parameter is `yes`. If `no` is not specified, sounds play out first.

An `interruptsound` parameter, again not shown in the examples, determines whether the sounds cut each other off or layer over each other. It defaults to `yes` (cut off), because according to the author, there is currently a bug either in Java or Netscape that cuts off *all* playing sounds whenever one of them finishes.

```
<param name="interruptsound" value="yes">
```

Two parameters you can use to establish paths to your audio and video files when you are using partial URLs are `usebase` and `custbase`. The values for both `usebase` and `custbase` are `document` and `code`. Usebase="document" resolves (completes) partial URLs from the document's URL. Usebase="code" resolves them from the location of the hibut.class file. The default is `usebase="document"`. Use `custbase` when you want a URL that isn't either of those. If `custbase` is relative, it will resolve the URL from the `usebase` parameter. You do not need to use either of these parameters if your media is in the same directory with the HTML document and class file. A full URL will override any `usebase` setting.

Use the parameter called URL to specify a URL to link to when the button is clicked. If none is supplied no link will take place. You can also specify a new browser window for the URL using the parameter `target`. The following line, for example, puts the page in a newly spawned browser window.

```
<param name="target" value="New Window 1">
```

You can name the button anything you like. This is useful when you are testing the parameters or have multiple buttons on the same page. When you give it a name and specify
the value yes with the parameter verbose, the applet outputs information relating to the
images it couldn't load, URL malformations, and so on, to a Java console in Netscape or
the Java Developers Kit. To access the console in Netscape simply select Show Java
Console under the Options menu. The default is no.

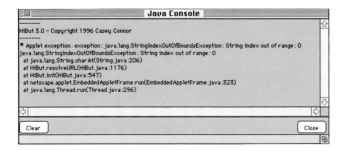

In the next example, three images are used to create a whimsical rollover animation of an
eye winking with accompanying sound (which you can hear by playing the applet on the
CD-ROM).

```
<applet code="HiBut.class" width="80" height="62">
<param name="normal" value="eye1.gif">
<param name="highlight" value="eye2.gif">
<param name="select" value="eye3.gif">
<param name="active" value="eye1.gif">
<param name="highlightsound" value="DoorSqueak.au">
<param name="selectsound" value="gasp.au">
<param name="activesound" value="UhOh.au">
<param name="highlightsoundloop" value="yes">
<param name="name" value="Eyeful">
</applet>
```

73

When the applet first starts to play, the eye is open. Moving the mouse over the image
changes it to an eye that is partially closed, and the sound of a creaking door is heard.
Clicking the image switches the image to an eye that is closed, and the sound changes to a
gasp. Releasing the mouse does not result in any visual changes because the image parameter was not changed, but the sound changes to a voice which says, "Uh oh." The only
code change was to substitute new images and sounds and change the size of the images.

The next example is simple animation with mouse-activated sound, which supplies an element of fun to a Web site.

```
<applet code="HiBut.class" width="28" height="65">
<param name=normal value="redlight.gif">
<param name=highlight value="redlight.gif">
<param name=select value="greenlight.gif">
<param name=active value="greenlight.gif">
<param name=normalsound value="GlassBreak.au">
<param name=highlightsound value="CarHorn.au">
<param name=selectsound value="TruckHorn.au">
<param name=activesound value="Screech.au">
<param name=highlightsoundloop value=yes>
<param name=name value="Varoom">
</applet>
```

When you move the mouse over the image of a red traffic light, you hear the sound of a single car horn. When you click the mouse, the light turns green and you hear the sound of a large truck horn. Releasing the mouse changes the sound of screeching tires. Moving the mouse away from the image results in the sound of breaking glass.

By reducing the number of assigned URLs, you also can use this applet to add a simple image with a sound file or a simple interactive image to your page. You also can use it to add background music or sound by giving your selected image URL a 1×1-pixel window size and no images, and have a normal sound clip looping.   ■

Interactive Imagemap

Applet: PicMap.class, mapPic.class, mapPicArrayLoader.class, StrExtract.class, ztl.class

PicMap offers a new way to do an imagemap. Instead of a single image with hot spots defined by coordinates, PicMap uses an image that is actually made up of a series of layered GIF images with transparent backgrounds. What appears to be one large image with hotspots actually includes several smaller, layered images, each of which acts as a button. PicMap can also show a reverse image when the button is clicked and float a text box where you can display a message when the mouse rolls over a button.

This approach enables you to create buttons with unusual shapes that would be impossible with a regular imagemap. The mouse messages attached to the buttons are another feature that is not available on many maps.

Another applet in a series by Hans Glitsch of Micro Nation Software (`http://www.flash.net/~hans/JavaCom/PicMap/PicMap.html`), PicMap shares some class files and commands with both "Scrolling Images" and "Twinkling Star." Five class files are required, including PicMap.class, mapPic.class, mapPicArrayLoader.class, StrExtract.class, and ztl.class. PicMap.class is the only one which must be referenced in the HTML document, but all must be present in the same folder to work.

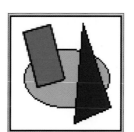

To make a map with this applet, first create the image you want to use for your imagemap as you normally would, then make one copy of the image for each button you want to create. Each copy will become a separate layer in your new multilayered imagemap.

Use an imaging program like Photoshop to crop out the parts you don't want to turn into a button on each layer. Now change everything else on the layer into a solid color, and make it transparent. Save each of the new layers as separate GIF files.

The new layers should be the same size as the original image with everything transparent except for your new buttons. Keep these new images in the same relative position as they were in the original so that the applet can seamlessly combine them with no overlapping.

In the examples shown, there are three hot spots: a red rectangle, a yellow oval, and blue triangle. Each one was constructed by copying the original image, cutting out everything except the area to be made into a button, and filling in the rest of the image with a solid white background. Any solid color will work as long as that color doesn't appear anywhere else in the image.

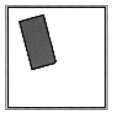  

If you want the "button down" or "pressed" state to be different, you can make yet another version of each image. For the sake of simplicity, the "down" versions here are illustrated by simply switching the colors. The down version of the rectangle is blue, the oval red, and the triangle yellow. When the applet is assembled, clicking the rectangle will change its color from red to blue.

  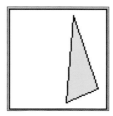

Use your graphic software to save the images as GIF89a files, which support transparency.

Here is the parameter set used to link everything in our example together:

```
<applet code="PicMap.class" width="140" height="100">
<param name="foreColor" value="000000">
<param name="backColor" value="FFFFFF">
<param name="backTileImage" value="anyback.jpg">
<param name="mousyMessFont" value="Helvetica,BoldItalic,14"> <param
name="mousyMessColor" value="FFFF00">
<param name="mousyMessBackColor" value="000000">


<param name="pic1" value="RectUp.gif">
<param name="pic1Down" value="RectDwn.gif">
<param name="pic1URL" value="http://www.anywhere.com">
<param name="pic1URLFrame" value="_self">
<param name="pic1MouseMessage" value="Rectangle">


<param name="pic2" value="OvalUp.gif">
<param name="pic2Down" value="OvalDwn.gif">
<param name="pic2URL" value="http://www.anotherplace.com">
<param name="pic2URLFrame" value="_self">
<param name="pic2MouseMessage" value="Oval">
```

```
<param name="pic3" value="TriUp.gif">
<param name="pic3Down" value="TriDwn.gif">
<param name="pic3URL" value="http://www.downunder.com">
<param name="pic3URLFrame" value="_self">
<param name="pic3MouseMessage" value="Triangle">
</applet>
```

In this example the images are all in the same directory as the HTML document and class files. Remember that if you have copied the class files into a directory other than the one that contains the HTML document, you must include a relative path to the class files.

The foreColor, and backColor settings are only used to determine the display that is seen while the applet is loading. The foreColor setting establishes the color of the message text, and backColor the background. The latter is also the default for the color of the background when no backTileImage is specified. Colors must be specified in hexadecimal format.

The optional backTileImage lets you establish a static image that is tiled behind everything else on the main window.

The MousyMess parameters are used to define the optional floating message box that opens above the imagemap when the user's mouse enters a button space. Here you can specify font characteristics and background color for the text you want to appear in the box. The floating box will move around on the image to follow the mouse pointer, and the text will change depending on which clickable area the mouse is over. If mousyMessBackColor is not specified, the text will be drawn directly over the images without a bounding rectangle.

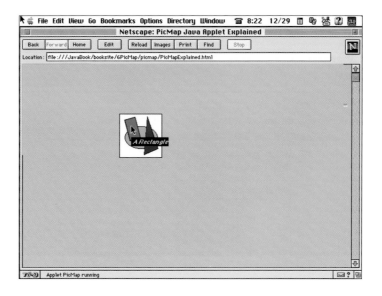

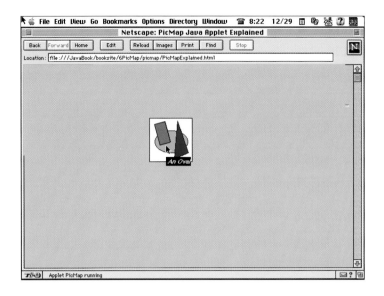

The setting pic1Down in the example shows how you specify an image to represent the "down" or "pressed" stage of the button click. Image files here are sent to the applet in the form of parameters pic1, pic2, and pic3. If there were more than three images, then you would simply continue with pic4, pic5, and so on. The integers in the parameters must start with 1 and increase by one without skipping.

Using pic1URL (2URL, 3URL, and so on.) you can specify the link for that hot spot. This can be a relative or full URL. You can also target a frame using the model pic1URLFrame.

Each hot spot can also have its own message in the message box. At pic1MouseMessage you can enter the text of any message you want displayed for that zone.

Working demos and a complete list of parameters are available from the Micro Nation Web site listed at the front of the chapter or the CD-ROM in the back of the book. These demo copies will work on your desktop but will require a registration number for the Web, which is available for $45 from the same Web site. ■

Audio Imagemap

Applets: dinkMap.class and dinkLink.class

DinkMap is the name of an applet by Matthew Roberts from Calvin College in Grand Rapids, Michigan, that adds button highlights and sounds to an imagemap.

Roberts started with the highlighting aspect of another applet by Rickard Oberg. He added the capability to play a sound file when the cursor enters a linked area and to display link information within the browser status window. He then christened his creation with the nickname of a friend at the college.

Imagemaps are a fixture on Web sites because of their capability to contain multiple hot spots on a photograph or drawing. Plotting the coordinates that determine the buttons or hot spots is a daunting task if done manually. A number of mapping tools, however, now exist to identify the coordinates and even write the code. DinkMap is no drag-and-drop map editor, but it does enable a couple of nice tricks.

In the example shown here from Roberts' Web page (`http://www.calvin.edu/~mrober57/`), when the user rolls the cursor over one of the headlines it activates a highlight effect and a sound bite. The highlight is a raised button image, and the audio file is a voice that describes the material linked to the button. Rolling the cursor over the author's name and email address produces another highlight effect. This time the letters change color and seem to glow.

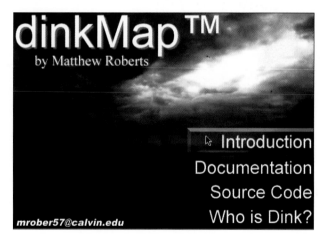

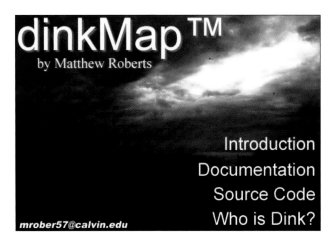

There are two images at work here. The basic screen is a photograph with text superimposed over the picture.

The second image is identical, except for the embossed effect that makes it look like a button and the highlight glow on Roberts' name and email address.

81

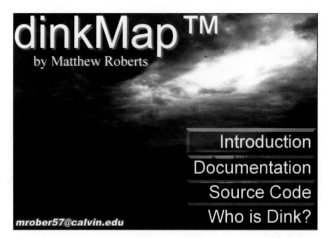

Note that this applet uses two class files, dinkMap.class and dinkLink.class. Both must be placed in the same folder, even though only dinkMap.class needs to be referenced from the HTML document.

Below is the parameter set Roberts used for the applet on his Web site. The number parameter following the references to the two images refers to the number of associated links in the imagemap, in this case 5. The three lines before Roberts' parameter set explain the formula he followed. Compare the link values in the formula to the actual parameter set to see what information is required and in what order:

```
<param name="link_x"
value="top_x,top_y,bottom_x,bottom_y,url_to_link_to,status_indicator,u
rl_of_sound OR nosound,frame_name OR noframe">
```

Roberts' code looks like this:

```
<applet code="dinkMap.class" width="521" height="360">
<param name="normal" value="dink.jpg">
<param name="highlight" VALUE="dink_hl.jpg">
<param name="number" value="5">
<param name="link1" value="297,191,521,238,dink_intro.html,
Introduction,introduction.au,_top">
<param name="link2" value="298,237,521,277,dink_doc.html,
Documentation,documentation.au,_top">
<param name="link3" value="298,278,521,315,dink_form.html,Source
Code,source_code.au,_top">
<param name="link4" value="297,315,521,358,dink_who.html,Who is
Dink?,who.au,_top">
<param name="link5" value="0,337,200,360,mailto:mrober57@calvin.edu,
Email Matthew Roberts,nosound,_top">
<map name="map">
<area shape="rect" coords="297,191,521,238" href="dink_intro.html">
<area shape="rect" coords="298,237,521,277" href="dink_doc.html">
```

```
<area shape="rect" coords="298,278,521,315" href="/dink_form.html">
<area shape="rect" coords="297,315,521,358" href="dink_who.html">
<area shape="rect" coords="0,337,200,360" href="mailto:
mrober57@calvin.edu">
</map>
<a href="/cgi-bin/imagemap/~mrober57/cgi-bin/dinkMap.map"><img
src="/~mrober57/Images/dink.jpg" alt="dinkMap v1.0, by Matthew Roberts"
usemap="#map" border="0" ismap></a>
</applet>
```

The value for the `normal` parameter is the name of the image you want displayed when nothing is highlighted. The value for the `highlight` parameter is the name of the image to be displayed when the user rolls the mouse over the applet.

Hot spots on an imagemap are defined by dividing the image into a graph and plotting X and Y coordinates that represent the relative shape and position of each button object with respect to the edges of the larger map. An object can be a rectangle, a circle, or a multi-sided polygon. X and Y coordinates for each hot spot show the distance down from the top and to the right of the upper-left-hand corner.

In our example, the parameter named `link1` lists the numbers "297,191,521,238." The first two numbers define the X and Y coordinates for the upper left-hand corner of the rectangular button image, which is 297 pixels to the right of the left border of the map and 191 pixels down from the top. The second two numbers define the coordinates for the lower right-hand corner of the same rectangle.

DinkMap requires that you enter the coordinates by hand, but the process is relatively painless because of another useful parameter you can activate to find or fine-tune the coordinates. Add the parameter below while you are working on your imagemap, and as you pass the mouse over the image the applet displays the X,Y mouse coordinates in the browser status window.

```
<param name="debug" value="yes">
```

83

In this example Roberts has included traditional imagemap instructions for visitors whose browsers can't run Java. The `<map></map>` section describes a basic client-side imagemap, where the end-user's computer connects the map coordinates with URLs. Roberts has also included a server-side imagemap (beginning with `<a href`) for older browsers that don't recognize client side maps. This approach relies on a call to a cgi script located on the server to match coordinates and URLs.

Although the sound files for DinkMap are all narrations, they could just as easily be music or effects tracks. The audio files must all be in .au format, the only audio format currently supported by Java.

Class files and source code for the applet are available on the book's CD-ROM or from the author. There have been problems in the past with accessing the server linked to his Web site. If you get an error message when trying to download code from the Web site, you may want to contact Roberts directly by email at mrober57@calvin.edu. ■

Rollover Imagemap

Applet: ActiveMap.class, ActiveMapLink.class

ActiveMap, from SenseNet (http://www.sensenet.com), is an applet that creates interactive imagemaps. Its usefulness, however, is not limited to making visual menus.

Often imagemaps are used as menus to navigate Web sites, but typically they consist of a single background graphic with hot spots linked to other pages. A visitor clicks the part of the image that links to the page where he or she wants to go.

With an ActiveMap imagemap you can add a highlight to a hot spot. For example, when the mouse rolls over the defined area, it triggers a new image or a text box. Actually clicking it triggers yet another action.

This makes navigation more fun and destinations clearer. It also means an ActiveMap imagemap can be much more than a navigational device. It can, for instance, provide your visitors with useful information in a graphical, interactive format. An imagemap can be an interactive roadmap.

In this example, rolling your mouse over one of the colored buttons on the map generates a new graphic at the top of the map with directions to your destination.

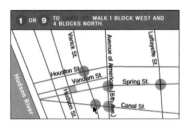

Here's the HTML code for this application:

```
<applet code="ActiveMap.class"
width="322" height="200">
<param name="background" value="
background.gif">
<param name="link1"
value="152,163,174,184">
<param name="link2"
value="178,166,199,188">
<param name="link3" value="131,102,151,123">
<param name="link4" value="276,125,298,146">
<param name="link5" value="176,128,198,151">
<param name="link6" value="111,139,127,152">
<param name="image1" value="0,0¦canal1.gif">
<param name="image2" value="0,0¦canalc.gif">
<param name="image3" value="0,0¦houston.gif">
<param name="image4" value="0,0¦spring6.gif">
<param name="image5" value="0,0¦springc.gif">
<param name="image6" value="0,0¦stop_by.gif">
</applet>
```

Two class files are needed: ActiveMap.class and ActiveMapLink.class. Both must reside in the same folder, but only ActiveMap.class is referenced in the HTML document. Here the class files are also in the same folder with the HTML document and image files. The image and class files could also have been in separate folders with specified paths.

The `background` parameter can utilize an image file, an RGB hex color, or both (in which case you need to separate them with the pipe character "|"). In the previous example, the background image is a map of a section of New York City.

The next set of parameters identifies the six links built into this map, as well as the X,Y coordinates that define the position of each hot spot or button in relation to the top and left margins of the map.

Here, for example, the parameter named `link1` lists the numbers 152,163,174,184 as coordinates. The first two numbers define the first set of X and Y coordinates for the lower red button image (which is 152 pixels to the right of the left border of the map, and 163 pixels down from the top). This point represents the upper-left-hand corner of the button, which is actually defined in the imagemap as a rectangle, even though it appears to be a circle. The second two numbers demarcate the lower-right-hand corner of the same button.

This program doesn't help you identify the coordinates. However, there are a number of mapping programs available that do—including MapEdit and MapThis for Windows and WebMap for the Macintosh. MapEdit is available on the CD-ROM that accompanies this book. The others can be downloaded from the Web.

With the coordinates for the links or button areas defined, it is time to assign and place the images that will appear when a visitor's cursor enters a button space. Note that the number of images must match the number of links and be in the same order—that is, `link1` must correspond to `image1`.

In this case `image1` is identified as `canal1.gif`, which offers directions to Canal Street.

In the HTML code, again there are X and Y coordinates for the location where the new graphic should appear when it is triggered. The value 0,0 means that the image appears at the extreme upper-left-hand corner of the applet. In this example, all of the instructions appear at this location. Each could appear at a separate location on the applet.

After the coordinates is the name of the image file that will appear at the designated location on the map.

All the action in the roadmap example takes place in mouse rollover mode. There is no link to another location when the visitor actually clicks the mouse. To create such a link you would add a URL to the `link` parameter, as you will see later in this chapter. You also could add a target frame or a status message to the same parameter.

In the next example ActiveMap is used to create an infographic, which is part of a tutorial for learning Spanish. The user is presented with an image with four Spanish words, each contained within a box. Each is the name of a familiar object.

Rolling the mouse over a word triggers a picture of the object named.

Clicking the mouse triggers a third image, which shows the English translation of the word.

Here's the HTML code:

```
<applet code="ActiveMap.class" height="66" width="258">
<param name="style" value="exclusive">
<param name="background" value=" spanish.gif">
<param name="active_image" value=" pictures.gif">
<param name="on_image" value=" english.gif">
<param name="link1" value="0,0,65,66">
<param name="link2" value="66,0,128,66">
<param name="link3" value="129,0,192,66">
<param name="link4" value="193,0,258,66">
</applet>
```

Notice there are no image parameters in the style of image1 here as in the previous example. This time the applet is accessing individual images on a larger graphic instead of a series of separate graphics. See the descriptions of active_image and on_image below for more information.

A new parameter is named style—set here as exclusive. This means that only one link at a time can be selected. The default or standard setting allows more than one open link; a useful option for games that could be created with this applet. In both cases, another click deselects the link. Other style settings are stayon, where a link remains selected once it is clicked; and stayactive, where a link remains highlighted after a mouse rollover. Primarily, these settings are intended to make more interesting games.

Also new in this example are two parameters called active_image and on-image, which like background define a specific function for an image. Here the background image is the strip of boxes that contain Spanish words described earlier.

The `active_image` is a strip of pictures in identical boxes, illustrating the objects named in the background panel. These appear box by box in sequence on mouse rollover, as illustrated earlier.

Clicking one of the pictures triggers an image from the `on-image` strip of boxes, which contains the English versions.

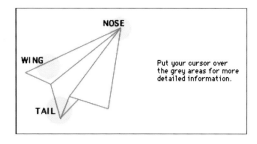

In the next example, ActiveMap triggers a series of text and picture pop-ups with explanatory information to help the user understand the demonstrated concept. The simple paper airplane used here could be replaced easily with a more sophisticated model.

Rolling over on one of the three designated information points brings up a box like this with a picture and a text description:

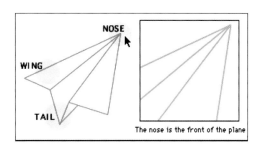

The nose is the front of the plane

The HTML code for this example looks like this:

```
<applet code="ActiveMap.class" width="380" height="166">
<param name="background" value="images_demo/plane/airplane.gif">
<param name="link1" value="118,12,155,143">
<param name="link2" value="26,60,60,91">
<param name="link3" value="40,116,73,149">
```

87

```
<param name="image1" value="166,10¦nose.gif">
<param name="text1" value="160,155¦The nose is the front of the
plane">
<param name="image2" value="166,10¦wing.gif">
<param name="text2" value="167,155¦The wing makes the plane fly">
<param name="image3" value="166,10¦tail.gif">
<param name="text3" value="164,155¦The tail is the back of the
plane">
</applet>
```

The `background` image here is the basic airplane image. The three links and related images are prepared like those in the first example. This time, however, the pop-up picture box is 166 pixels to the right of the left border, and 10 pixels down from the top.

Another change is the line of text, which is programmed to appear with each of the numbered images. The text that accompanies each image is described in the `text` parameters. These must correspond in number and order to the links and image. The `text1` parameter, for example, is coded to appear at 160 pixels across and 155 down onscreen, which is just outside the parameter of the picture box. The wording for each message appears on the same line after the coordinates and separated by a pipe symbol ("|"). The value for `text1`, for example, is `The nose is the front of the plane`.

The final example in this chapter is an imagemap for the company that makes this applet. It serves as both a menu and an information source.

When the mouse enters the area occupied by the image, three headings pop up, which link to different sections (Technology, Company, and Solutions) on the company Web site.

Each of the headings is also a trigger. Rolling the mouse over the headings reveals additional pop-up image messages that are displayed in the center of the picture in place of the company logo.

```
<applet codebase="classes" code="ActiveMap.class" width="235" height="235">
<param name="style" value="exclusive">
<param name="background" value="background.gif">
<param name="link1" value="0,0,234,234">
<param name="link2" value="72,10,160,76¦http://www.sensenet.com/tech">
<param name="link3" value="22,126,88,188¦http://www.sensenet.com/inc">
<param name="link4" value="148,128,216,190¦http://www.sensenet.com/solu-
tions">
<param name="image1" value="30,30¦stay_active.gif">
<param name="image2" value="67,93¦tech_on.gif">
<param name="image3" value="67,93¦company_on.gif">
<param name="image4" value="64,92¦solutions_on.gif">
</applet>
```

Although this map looks quite different from the others shown, the parameters are very similar. The biggest difference is that the buttons are linked to URLs via link parameters.

Using other ActiveMap parameters (not shown in any of the examples here) you can specify frames to display URLs. A global frame parameter assigns all links to appear in a selected frame. Here the target is a new browser window.

```
<param name="frame" value="_blank">
```

You can assign a specific link to a specific frame by using the link parameter. You can also display a message in the Browser's status line. The frame assignment is the third variable in the link parameter command line, after the X,Y coordinates and URL. The status message is variable number four. The last three variables are all optional. When used they are separated by the pipe symbol "|". Also, blank fields must be included if you want to specify the last field. Here's what this would look like.

```
<param name="link3" value="22,126,88,188¦http://www.sensenet.com/inc¦
_blank¦this is a status line">
```

Demo versions of the ActiveMap class files, which can be used locally on your own computer, can be found on the CD-ROM in the back of this book, or at the Sensenet Web site. To use the applet on the Web you must register each site, where you intend to use it, and pay a license fee of $49 per site. ∎

89

Dynamic Billboard

Applet: DynamicBillBoard.class, BillData.class, BillTransition.class, ColumnTransition.class, FadeTransition.class, LargeImageFadeTransition.class, RotateTransition.class, SmashTransition.class, TearTransition.class, UnrollTransition.class

You have seen this applet, by Robert Temple, Embry-Riddle Aeronautical University of Bunnell, Florida (`http://www.db.erau.edu`), used quite a few places on the Web for advertising. It shows a series of same-size images for a specified time period. Each image is a hyperlink to a URL; when a Web site visitor clicks an image, his or her browser goes to the URL specified.

> **Tango Foot Powder**
>
> 10oz. Can $4.95

Setting up this flexible applet on a Web page is straightforward:

```
<applet code="DynamicBillBoard.class" width="#" height="#">
<param name="delay" value="#">
<param name="billboards" value="#">
<param name="bill0" value="x.gif,http://y,z">
<param name="bill1" value="x.gif,http://y,z">
<param name="bill2" value="x.gif,http://y,z">
<param name="bill3" value="x.gif,http://y,z">
<param name="transitions" value="#,x,y,z">
<param name="bgcolor" value="#">
</applet>
```

For bills:

- ■ `x` is the billboard image
- ■ `y` is the URL to which the image is linked
- ■ `z` is the text to go in the browser status line

For transitions:

- ■ `x`, `y`, and `z` are transitions

The `width` and `height` attributes set the size for all images, which must be GIFs or JPEGs—all the same size. A typical size for advertising banners is about 460×60 pixels.

The `delay` parameter sets the display time for each image in milliseconds. Remember, there are 1,000 milliseconds per second. The entry for five seconds is 5,000.

The `billboards` parameter specifies the number of images used. For five images, the entry is 5.

You must enter a parameter statement for each image. If you use five images, you must enter five parameter statements (for example, `bill0`, `bill1`, `bill2`, `bill3`, and `bill4`). The last image number (`bill4`) is one less than the total number of images (five) because the first image is `bill0`.

The value for the `bill` parameters consists of three inputs separated by commas. The first is the name of the image file (`tigerbalm.gif`, for example). The second is the URL for which the image acts as a hyperlink (`http://www.balmco.com`, for example). The third (which is optional) is a string of text that will appear on the status bar of the browser when a visitor moves his or her mouse over the billboard (for example, `Use Tigerbalm for aching muscles.`).

The value for the transitions-between-graphics parameter starts with the number of types of transitions used, followed by a comma, and then followed by the name of each transition separated by commas. There can be no spaces in the entry. For instance, `2,FadeTransition,UnrollTransition` is a valid entry.

Finally, the value for the background color `bcolor` is the hexadecimal number for the color.

This applet loads color images (billboards) quickly and it loads images and classes only when needed. Thus, it runs efficiently. Each transition removes the current image and replaces it with the succeeding image. Each transition method is a separate class:

- ■ `ColumnTransition`: The current image together with the succeeding image turns into a shutter-like display. The shutter display is then followed by the entire succeeding image.

- ■ `FadeTransition`: The current image fades out, and the succeeding image fades in.

- ■ `RotateTransition`: The current image appears to rotate out of visibility on a rectangular bar, and the succeeding image appears to rotate in.

- ■ `SmashTransition`: This is similar to the Fade, but with a more coarse granularity.

- ■ `TearTransition`: The current image is torn away, revealing the succeeding image underneath.

- ■ `UnrollTransition`: The succeeding image rolls out over the current image.

The Dynamic Billboard operates randomly. It selects the first and all succeeding images randomly, as well as all transitions. It just keeps going and going.

You store the graphics with the classes (or include a path to the directory where stored). You can easily add or delete graphics from the billboard. Following are four GIFs for a Dynamic Billboard presentation followed by the requisite `applet` statement.

```
<applet code="DynamicBillBoard.class" width="250" height="136">
<param name="delay" value="1000">
<param name="billboards" value="4">
<param name="bill0" value="bb.gif,http://www.bb.com,Them Bobby
Burgers sure are good!">
<param name="bill1" value="bc.gif,http://www.bookcenter.com,See the
BookCenter for fine books!">
<param name="bill2" value="cc.gif,http://www.cc.com,Twice the kick of
other leading colas.">
<param name="bill3" value="ad.gif,http://www.dybillboard.com,Makes
advertising sense."> -- -- -- --
<param name="transitions"
value="6,ColumnTransition,FadeTransition,TearTransition,SmashTransition,
UnrollTransition,RotateTransition">
<param name="bgcolor" value="#FFFFFF">
</applet>
```

Set up this way, the applet displays as a rectangle on the Web page. Note the message on the status bar at the bottom of the browser.

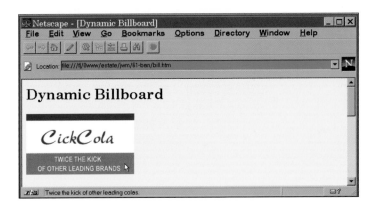

You can dress up this applet with a few GIFs.

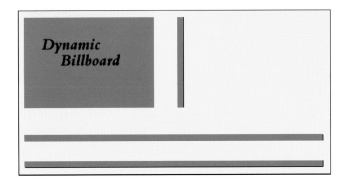

When they go together, they look more attractive.

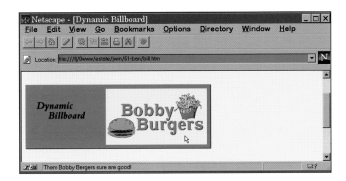

As another example, the University Web site displays the applet inside a head graphic (on the right side). Notice how the head graphic wraps around the applet.

Outside magazine uses another approach. The applet was added to the right side of the head graphic, making it appear to be part of the head graphic without wrapping it. Can you tell where the head graphic ends and the applet starts? ■

Chat: The Fog

Applet: FogApplet.class, FogEntry.class, FogPanel.class, FogPlate.class, FogSlider.class

The Fog, a Java chat applet developed by Hannes Wallnofer of Vienna, Austria (http://www.t0.or.at:7272/fog.html or http://www.t0.or.at/~hwallnoefer/download.html), presents a unique appearance. Each participant chooses a color. A participant's chat text appears onscreen within a color bar of the selected color. Simply clicking somewhere in the frame, typing a line of text, and pushing the Enter or Return key is how you start chatting. Participants also can choose where on the chat screen they want their text to appear, presumably close to the person with whom they are chatting.

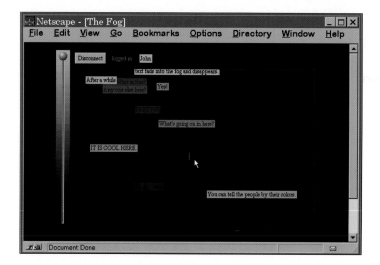

This applet also includes a larger version of The Fog, which takes up a huge amount of space on a monitor (not shown).

As you can see, this chat applet is more conducive to socializing than business. The Fog server does not keep a record of the chat sessions, but it does maintain the last 15 entries in memory. An entry is a bright color at first. As subsequent entries are made, the color fades. When it becomes the sixteenth entry, it finally disappears—that is, it gets lost in the fog.

A participant chooses a color by moving a ball up and down the color rod. The rod changes color as the participant moves the ball. The color of the rod is the participant's color. A participant should choose a color that is not in use.

A participant can enter his or her nickname too. Clicking Go enables a participant to enter The Fog and participate.

Although using The Fog is straightforward, you will need to provide instructions to your Web site visitors on how to participate. The developer provides an instruction page that you can use or modify.

You install this applet in a Web page with the following applet statement. You can change the foreground and background colors of the applet by using the parameters fgcolor and bgcolor, respectively. Color values must be in hex notation.

```
<applet code="FogApplet.class" width="550" height="350">
<param name="port" value="7234">
<param name="bgcolor" value="5CADAD">
<param name="fgcolor" value="222222">
</applet>
```

95

The applet Java classes are in a subdirectory (subfolder) named fogapplet.

The only catch to using this applet is that you must run The Fog server with the Web server on your server computer to make the client work. Setting up the server is beyond the scope of this book, but installation is easy. A Java interpreter (from the Java SDK) must be installed. If you installed your Web server, you will find setting up this chat server a simple task. If you depend on someone else to run your Web server (such as an Internet Service Provider), the installation of The Fog will be a minor task for them. All the Java classes that comprise the server are included with The Fog software and are in a subdirectory named fogserver. The developer of The Fog provides detailed installation instructions. The chat server should reside on the same computer as the Web server, and the `port` parameter shown previously indicates the port to be used. ■

Live Chat

Applet: JavaTalkClient.class, Listener.class, Typist.class

Francesco Stajano of the Olivetti and Oracle Research Laboratory of Cambridge, United Kingdom, (`http://badges.cam-orl.co.uk/~fms/javatalk/`) has developed JavaTalk chat software that is simple but useful.

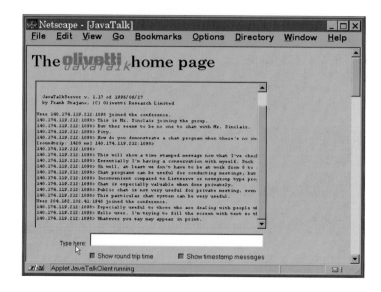

```
<applet code="JavaTalkClient.class" width="511" height="377">
<param name="port" value="6764">
<param name="host" value="bookcenter.com">
<param name="showRoundTrip" value="false">
<param name="showTimestamps" value="false">
</applet>
```

A chat participant types his or her text and pushes the Enter (or Return on a Mac) key to post it in the chat frame. Participants are identified by their IP numbers, unless they execute (type) the MYNAME command in the Type here entry form, followed by their name. Each participant's text is placed in the chat frame in the order it's received. Unfortunately, there appears to be no word wrap. That means every participant has only one line. It keeps the conversation going better perhaps, but it makes long lines inconvenient to read. Additionally, the print is small. Nonetheless, it is easy to understand how you can use this chat productively in a variety of situations. This chat device has a no-nonsense attitude. In fact, the developer had online meetings in mind when he developed this system, not casual socializing. The Java classes for the applet are in a subdirectory (subfolder) named client (see the CD-ROM).

The two checkboxes that appear below the chat frame and the `showRoundTrip` and `showTimestamps` parameters are of interest only to programmers. The applet's creator intends to remove them in future versions.

One important feature of this applet is the log, which permanently records all chat sessions. Thus, you can email a transcript of the session to all participants. This feature is a plus for those holding meetings or conducting business via JavaTalk and is part of the JavaTalk server.

The JavaTalk logo is not part of the applet and is added with HTML. You can easily replace it with your own graphic.

The drawback of all chat systems is that they require servers. JavaTalk is no exception. The JavaTalk chat server, which is a Java applet, must run on the same server computer as the Web server. A Java interpreter (in the Java SDK) must be running on the computer too. The developer has provided explicit installation instructions for the server, and installation is not difficult (although beyond the scope of this book). If you do not tend the computer that runs your Web server, the person who does tend it should have no trouble installing the JavaTalk server. The server files are in the subdirectory named server. The `port` parameter is the number of the port on which the JavaTalk server runs; the `host` parameter is for the URL of the server computer.

 If you cannot run this applet at a permanent Web site, you still can use the JavaTalk server for meetings. You can set up a Web server such as O'Reilly & Associates' WebSite in Windows 95 or Windows NT on your PC, which is easy to do. Run it temporarily using your Internet dial-up connection and have friends, colleagues, clients, or vendors join you for a chat (a meeting). You will need to provide your participants with your IP address in numerical form (for example, 214.17.512.45). Your Internet Service Provider probably uses dynamic IP addresses. Consequently, you will not know your IP address until *after* you get online for the meeting, at which time you will need to notify the other participants with your IP address. Try it. The toughest part is not the software—it's getting everyone online at the same time. ■

Clocks

Clocks provide time and date information obtained from the clock of a Web site visitor's computer. This chapter gives examples of both analog and digital (text) clocks. A text clock makes a nice accommodation for your Web site visitors, particularly in places where it is useful to them. Using text, you can make the time/date information blend into the Web page (it's there when readers need it, but it's otherwise unobtrusive). Or, you can make the time/date part of a more colorful graphical design where it actively competes for visitors' attention.

Analog Clock

Applet: Clock2.class

The analog clock applet provides a graphic in motion. It publishes the time information provided by a Web site visitor's computer in the traditional clock format. It also provides the date and a digital expression of the current time.

You can change the color parameters for the background and the two colors for the clock. Otherwise, this applet doesn't have much flexibility. There is no point in changing the dimensions of this applet, as the clock does not resize.

```
<applet code="Clock2.class" width="170" height="170">
<param name="bgcolor" value="000000">
<param name="fgcolor1" value="ff0000">
<param name="fgcolor2" value="ff00ff">
</applet>
```

Changing the colors, however, may help you adapt the clock to your Web page (on using hex numbers, see "Getting Started"). For instance, changing the background color to match the background of your Web page makes the clock blend in well with your page, while providing the time clearly.

After you have adjusted the background color, you may need to adjust the two clock colors (foreground colors) for proper contrast and greater clarity.

This analog clock was developed by Rachel Gollub, Sun Microsystems, Inc. of Mountain View, California, (`http://www.javasoft.com/applets/applets/Clock/`), and is the basis for the following text.

Text Clock

Applet: Clock2.class

Perhaps a more useful rendition of the clock is this digital version, which is easy to embed in the text of a Web document. This text clock was developed by Per Reedtz Thomsen, Netscape Communications, of Mountain View, California (`http://www.netscape.com/people/pthomsen/clock/`).

```
<applet code="Clock2.class" width="275" height="30">
<param name="FontFamily" value="Courier">
<param name="FontSize" value="18">
<param name="DateFmt" value="%c">
<param name="BGCol" value="f0f0f0">
</applet>
```

As before, the first step is to change the applet background to match the background of the Web page. Do this via the `BGCol` parameter.

> 11/30/96 20:23:55

Using the `FontFamily` and `FontSize` parameters, you can change the typeface and size to match the text in the Web page or to create a desired effect.

> 11/30/96 20:25:00

You can also add a parameter for font weight (values include bold and italic) and one for font (foreground) color too.

> **11/30/96 20:31:16**

```
<param name="FontWeight" value="bold">
<param name="FGCol" value="000000">
```

One of the most important parameters is `DateFmt`, the format for the time and date. You can select from 23 formatting elements to create almost any standard expression of the time and date (see the details on the CD-ROM).

Next, try moving the text clock to different positions in your Web page where it may work effectively but is integrated inconspicuously into the text.

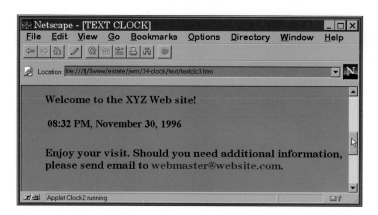

Changing the typeface size and positioning the applet under a heading graphic gives it a certain prominence without making it too distracting.

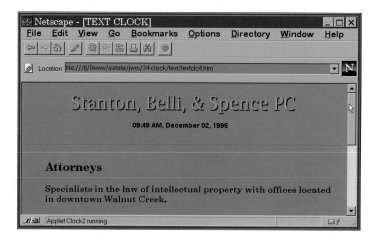

Or, you might try integrating the applet into a sentence in a paragraph, keeping in mind that you have no control over the font or font size in a Web site visitor's browser. For many Web sites, however, a more colorful approach is in order. By changing the background color, the font color, the font size, the time/date expression, and the dimensions, you can give the clock many different looks. ■

Counter

Applet: BeanCounter.class

Adam Bennie (http://www.ontonet.be/beancounter/beanc.html) created BeanCounter. It's not something every Web site needs, but it may prove an attractive addition to the sites of those Webmasters who can put it to use.

Bobby Burgers fast food competes well against the national franchises. On its Web site, it wants to show all the hamburgers it has sold and wants the number to be up-to-date. BeanCounter is an easy-to-use applet for doing so. You provide the starting number, start date, and rate of increase, and BeanCounter does the rest.

```
<applet codebase="BeanCounter" code="BeanCounter.class" width="120"
height="30">
<param name="startvalue" value="1010445">
<param name="startdate" value="1 Jan 1996 0:0:1 GMT">
<param name="increment" value="1 0:0:2:41:500">
<param name="bgcolor" value="FFFF99">
<param name="bordercolor" value="FFFF99">
<param name="textcolor" value="3399CC">
<param name="fontfile" value="../Fonts/odometer.gif">
<param name="border" value="0,flat">
<param name="align" value="center, bottom">
</applet>
```

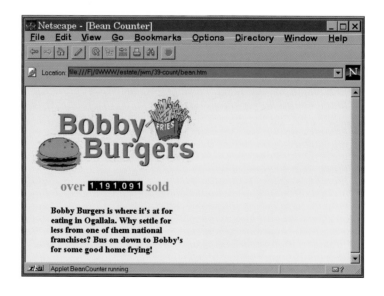

There are plenty of parameters to give you a lot of flexibility in controlling the look of this applet on your Web page (see the CD-ROM for complete details). You can make it shout, or you can even incorporate it subtly into the text on your Web page. For instance, to make an attractive counter without a graphic font, substitute the `font` parameter in place of the `fontfile` parameter in order to use normal fonts.

```
<param name="font" value="TimesRoman, bold, 20">
```

Use Times Roman, Helvetica, or Courier, as those are the only fonts that *every* PC and Mac user has installed. The styles are plain, bold, and italic. Set the background color to dark blue and the text color to yellow.

```
<param name="bgcolor" value="0000A0">
<param name="textcolor" value="FFFF00">
```

Then set the border to be five pixels wide with a bevel shape and a dusty canyon rosé color.

```
<param name="border" value="5,bevel">
<param name="bordercolor" value="D08080">
```

Now you have counter that you have created without a graphic font.

The applet also comes with five interesting graphic fonts that you can put to use immediately.

Additionally, you can create your own graphic fonts. It's simple to do. Your graphic (GIF) must contain 14 identically sized horizontal spaces. A sequential number starting with 0 goes in each of the first 10 spaces. The eleventh space contains a hyphen. The twelfth space contains a comma, which must be in the first left-hand one-third of that space. Leave the last two spaces blank. When you get through designing your own graphic font per the diagram below, it should look like the graphic fonts shown above.

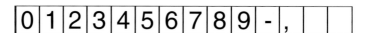

Your GIF is now complete. BeanCounter displays your numbers using the graphic font you created. This makes custom work not only possible, but reasonably easy.

TIP **Make the background of your graphic font transparent for additional flexibility. If the background color of the applet is the same as the background color of the Web page, the numbers *float* on the Web page.**

Bobby Burgers (first illustration) shows the odometer font without a border, but you can use the `border` parameter to create six different borders in an unlimited variety of widths and colors. Border values include:

- `flat`
- `raise`
- `lower`
- `bevel`
- `chisel`
- `emboss`

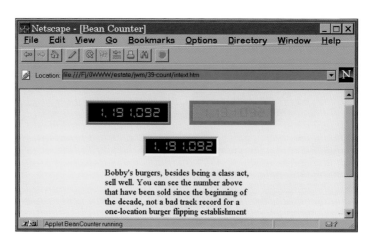

Perhaps the most difficult part of using BeanCounter is determining the rate of increase (the `increment` parameter); that is, the number increase per time unit. For Bobby Burgers, it was a matter of simply dividing the 1995 sales (195,260) by the numbers of hours in a year (8,760) to estimate a rate of 22.29 Bobby Burgers per hour, or one Bobby Burger each 2 minutes 41.5 seconds.

```
<param name="increment" value="1 0:0:2:41:500">
```

You can update the `increment` together with the starting number (`startvalue`: 1,010,445 for Bobby Burgers) and starting date (`startdate`: January 1, 1996 for Bobby Burgers) as often as you need to in order to publish acceptably accurate numbers.

```
<param name="startvalue" value="1010445">
<param name="startdate" value="1 Jan 1996 0:0:1 GMT"> ■
```

Visitor Counter

Applet: Counter.class

Many of the counters of Web site visitors require that you install CGI scripts or other software on the Web server computer. Cam's Dynamic Counter applet works on a Web site that the developer, Cameron Gregory of Red Bank, New Jersey (`http://www.local.com/counter/`), has set up for you. You simply make a reference to his Web site and the applet (in the `applet` statement in your Web page), and the counter magically works for your Web page. Unfortunately, it only counts visitors with Java-enabled Web browsers, but those undoubtedly constitute a substantial portion of Web users.

To use this applet, you simply put the following statement in your Web page:

```
<applet archive="http://www.local.com/counter/Counter.zip"
codebase="http://www.local.com/counter/" code="Counter.class"
width="75" height="20">

<param name="URL" value="http://www.yourURL.com/yourdirectory
yourWebpage.html">

</applet>
```

The important thing to remember is that you substitute your URL, your directory, and your Web page in the `param`. For instance, if your domain is `www.rabbits.com` and the Web page where you want the counter is `warrens.html` in the directory (folder) `michigan`, which is a subdirectory of your Web root directory, the parameter would be as follows:

```
<param name="URL" value="http://www.rabbits.com/michigan/
warrens.html">
```

Each time a visitor with a Java-enabled Web browser visits the Web page warrens.html, it communicates to the counter at `www.local.com` (Mr. Gregory's Web server), which keeps a visitor count. The counter then communicates the running total to a graphic representation of the counter on your warrens.html Web page. The graphic looks like an odometer.

00012 You also can add text to it.

00018 people have visited this Web site since December 10, 1996.

An additional parameter, `img`, enables you to change the image sets that make up the counter graphic. (The default.gif white on black is shown here.)

```
<param name="img" value="http://www.local.com/counter/default.gif">
```

The additional image sets available are as follows:

```
default-white-black.gif
default-black-blue.gif
default-black-green.gif
default-black-green2.gif
default-black-red.gif
```

The `noinc` parameter enables you to monitor your visitor count without adding to the count. In other words, it publishes the odometer image on another Web page (`monitor.html`, for example), but the visits to that page will not add to the visitor count. This must be used with the `url` parameter, which specifies the Web page where the count is being conducted. When value equals `true`, `noinc` is on and the count at the specified URL is monitored. Using the applet with the parameters below, from any Web page you can monitor the visitor count at art965.html at the BookCenter without adding to the visitor count at art965.html.

```
<param name="url" value="http://www.bookcenter.com/reporter/art965.html">
<param name="noinc" value="true">
```

This applet illustrates how you can use an applet at another URL as if it were on your server computer. What great magic! The following attribute from the `applet` statement enables such a connection:

```
codebase="http://www.local.com/counter/"
```

What it boils down to is that Mr. Gregory provides a service to you at no cost to you. If his server is down and your counter is temporarily inoperable, well, you can't complain too loudly. Eventually, Mr. Gregory expects to make available the source code for the counter server that runs at `www.local.com`. With the source code, you can install the counter server on your Web server computer, if you have the requisite access. ■

Calculator

Applet: PocketCalc.class, CalcButton.class, CalcFrame.class

This simple calculator provides visitors with a valuable convenience for situations in which they need to make a calculation at your Web site. This Java applet is a good example of a workhorse Java application. Mike Bonnier of Lund, Sweden (`http://www.df.lth.se/~mikaelb/pocketcalc-enu.shtml`) created it. Although not dramatic, it shows the power of embedded programming. Keep in mind that the capability to include embedded programming in a digital document is one of the leading features of multimedia authoring and the Web provides a powerful multi-media publishing system.

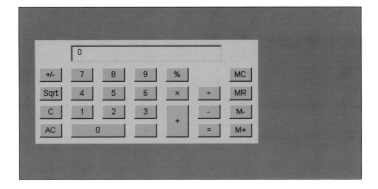

```
<applet code="PocketCalc.class" width="395" height="179">
</applet>
```

You can change the dimensions of the calculator as defined by the background color, but such a change merely adds area to the bottom and right side of the calculator.

To include this calculator in a Web page may unduly burden a visitor's computer and add more waiting time for the Web page to load. Therefore, provide the calculator only where it is a necessary convenience. As an alternative, embed a hyperlink in your Web page to enable a visitor to jump to the calculator when needed. The hyperlink takes the visitor to another Web page where the calculator is embedded. For instance, the hyperlink might be a calculator icon.

When a visitor clicks on the hyperlink (calculator icon), it takes him or her to a special Web page that contains the calculator and nothing more. Note that you can set the calculator background to match the Web page color using the BGCOLOR parameter, thus creating a pleasant visual effect. (Note that colors are defined in hexadecimal notation; see "Getting Started" for details.)

```
<param name="BGCOLOR" value=#FFC1C0">
```

Add a label ("Calculator," for example), and you've installed a functional and attractive calculator.

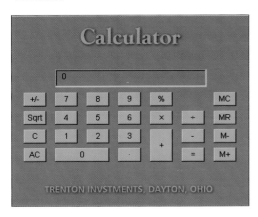

Unfortunately, the operating system color settings of the visitor's computer set the color for the calculator buttons. Thus, you have no control over the appearance of the buttons.

As an alternative, provide a button applet (see "Rollover Button") to enable a visitor to call up the calculator on another Web page. Unfortunately, the button program itself is a Java applet and, therefore, may not give a visitor much of a resource or time savings over the calculator applet at the time the Web page containing the button loads. ∎

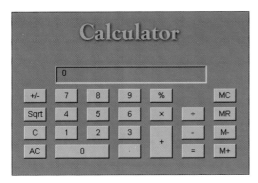

Loan Calculator

Applet: Interest.class

Embedded programs in Web pages prove useful now and will in the future to provide a service or convenience to visitors. Most of these embedded programs are highly specialized—designed specifically for the business at hand. This chapter features a general loan calculator, as an example that everyone can understand. Unfortunately, this is a no-frills applet. It comes only in gray. Nonetheless, it's useful. Robert J. Johnson, Hypertech Media of Tustin, California (`http://hypertechmedia.com/Interest.html`), has done a good job with this applet, and it will make a useful addition to your Web site.

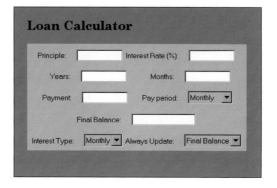

You use the Java file Interest.class with a simple HTML markup.

```
<applet code="Interest.class" width="420" height="230">
</applet>
```

There's not much to installing it. The story does not end here, however. You need to ask two questions:

- What can you do to dress up this applet?

- What information must you provide to assist Web site visitors in using it?

The first question has at least one simple answer: Make an attractive heading for the applet.

Loan Calculator

Put the heading together with the applet and your Web page is a little brighter. Use your artistic imagination when installing applets—even for intranets.

Loan Calculator

Principle: [ ]   Interest Rate (%): [ ]

Years: [ ]   Months: [ ]

Payment: [ ]   Pay period: [Monthly ▼]

Final Balance: [ ]

Interest Type: [Monthly ▼]   Always Update: [Final Balance ▼]

The second question presents more arduous considerations. How much information is enough, and how do you present it? The loan calculator is simple enough. Even so, most people need to be taught how to use it and what they can accomplish with it. If your Web site caters to financial professionals, one or two paragraphs may be enough. If it caters to college graduates, three or four paragraphs may be enough; if it caters to middle school students, you may have to provide several Web pages of instruction.

As simple as this calculator seems, it is a powerful tool for discounted cash flow analysis comparable to a financial calculator used by financial professionals. So, dress it up a little with some access to the instructions that are appropriate for the visitors to your Web site. Note that you can hyperlink each word (MORTGAGE, for example) to anchors, in the same Web page, or to other Web pages that contain the appropriate instructions for your visitors. ■

Netscape - [file:///f | /0www/estate/jwm/41-int/int2.htm]

File   Edit   View   Go   Bookmarks   Options   Directory   Window   Help

Location: file:///f|/0www/estate/jwm/41-int/int2.htm

Loan Calculator

Principle: [95000]   Interest Rate (%): [8.25]

Years: [30]   Months: [0]

Payment: [-708.83]   Pay period: [Monthly ▼]

Final Balance: [0]

Interest Type: [Monthly ▼]   Always Update: [Payment ▼]

INSTRUCTIONS

MORTGAGE

AUTO LOAN

AUTO LEASE

113

Currency Converter

Applet: Converter.class

The currency converter is another example of an embedded program that can prove to be quite a convenience to visitors of appropriate Web sites (travel Web sites, for example). This applet was developed by Wilfred Boayue Jr. (http:// members.tripod.com/~boayue/Converter.html). To use the applet, you enter the amount for one currency and that amount when converted to another currency then displays.

The conversion rates go in a text file called rates.dat, which you will need to update as often as is appropriate for your particular use. Here is a portion of rates.dat:

```
Argentina#0.9988
Australia#1.2666
Austria#10.46
Belgium#30.45
Brazil#1.0168
```

Each number refers to a value relative to the U.S. dollar. If you need an ongoing update, look on the Web for a currency conversion applet that communicates directly with an online information source that provides the current rates. Visit http://cnnfn.com/markets/currencies.html for current currency conversion rates.

This applet needs more dressing up than most. You can't even change its color. However, you can put a border around it easily enough by positioning graphics above it, below it, and on each side. The applet area is set at 480×80 pixels. If you want to put a 10-pixel border around the applet, use solid-color rectangular graphics as follows: upper and lower GIFs equal 500×10 pixels, and right and left GIFs equal 10×80 pixels.

Note that in this example, upper and lower GIFs are identical, as are the right and left GIFs. The HTML for the border is straightforward.

```
<img src="upper.gif"><br>
<img src="right.gif"><applet code="Converter.class" width="480"
height="80">
<param name="rates" value="rates.dat">
</applet><img src="left.gif"><br>
<img src="lower.gif" align="top">
```

You get the idea. Now try something more elaborate. In the next version, the upper and lower GIFs are 480×10 pixels, and the additional blue square GIF is 20×20 pixels. A 10×80 pixels, one-color transparent GIF is placed on the right side of the applet.

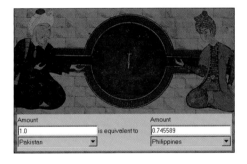

```
<img src="blue.gif"><img src="upper.gif"><img src="blue.gif"><br>
<img src="transgif.gif"><img src="right.gif"><applet code="Converter.class"
width="480" height="80">
<param name="rates" value="rates.dat">
</applet><img src="left.gif"><br>
<img src="blue.gif"><img src="lower.gif" align="top"><img src="blue.gif">
```

Or, you can add art for a more elegant effect.

This version requires pasting together strips from a digital rendering of an antique Arabic tile.

```
<img src="arabtile.jpg"><br>
<img src="stile.jpg"><applet
code="Converter.class" width="480"
height="80">
<param name="rates" value=
"rates.dat">
</applet><img src="stile.jpg"><br>
<img src="btile.jpg"> ■
```

115

Product Ordering

Applet: SafeOrderWindow.class, ProductWindow.class, MesBox.class, Globals.class, DigFrame.class, Client.class

Are you selling something on the Web and need a safe ordering system for your customers? You can use the SafeOrder applet (http://www.inside.net/SafeOrder/) developed by INside of Indermuehle, Switzerland to provide your customers with a secure device for purchasing. SafeOrder is a Java applet that encrypts an order (including credit card numbers) before transmission. The order is sent to you via email or directly to your Web server. You use a decoder (not covered in this chapter) to decode the encoded message you receive. The customer simply fills in his or her order, credit information, and clicks the Send button.

```
<applet code="SafeOrderWindow.class" width="580" height="619">
<param name="settings" value="SafeOrder.settings">
</applet>
```

Why do you need SafeOrder for selling? A substantial portion of your potential customers are behind firewalls where they may not be able to use the encryption system built into the leading Web browsers. Some potential customers are not concerned about security, but many are worried. SafeOrder assures concerned customers that their credit card information is safe as it moves across the Internet.

In addition, SafeOrder makes a handy ordering device. Why reinvent the wheel? Use SafeOrder or a comparable ready-made Java applet rather than program your own order form. (In fact, you can set up SafeOrder so that it does not take credit cards but acts purely as an ordering form.) SafeOrder enables you to customize the order form. It even lets you put in your own title graphic (in other words, replace the SafeOrder logo), show products, and play audio clips.

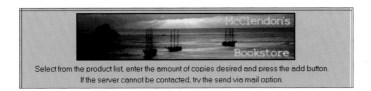

Because customizing SafeOrder is—in essence—creating your order form, it takes a little work. You do it, however, in plain text—without having to know any Java programming. The result is a custom order form that you can update easily as your business requires.

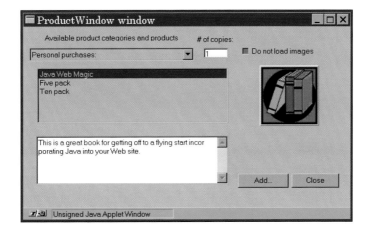

To customize SafeOrder, you use two text files: SafeOrder.settings for basic settings and products.list for products. The settings file includes such information as currency (dollar, lira, peso, yuan, and so on), credit cards accepted, sales tax, and shipping and is about two pages long (check one out on the CD-ROM). Note that SafeOrder can be read in four languages: English, German, French, and Italian.

117

The product file is simple to make, but you must create it carefully, as the text and grammar must be precise. The product file for the previous order form looks like this:

```
//This can be a comment line.

Personal purchases:
Java Web Magic:This is a great book for getting off to a flying
start incorporating Java into your Web site.:35.00:book.jpg
Five pack:Computer books make excellent gifts for Christmas,
Valentine's Day, and Halloween.:166.00:gift2.jpg
Ten pack:For those with many boyfriends, girlfriends, husbands,
wives, or all of the above. Remember Valentine's Day:322.00:heart.jpg

Corporate purchases:
Java Web Magic:This is a great book for getting off to a flying
start incorporating Java into your Web site. Every employee will want
a copy:35.00:book.jpg
Twenty pack:This pack will bring most small business up to speed on
enhancing their Web sites.:630.00:twenty.jpg
Hundred pack:If your company is serious about being competitive, this
is the pack for you. Order three or four today.:3080.00:hundred.jpg
```

Save the file as plain text (without line breaks). Make sure that the graphic files are JPEGs, they exist, and they are in the same directory as the Web page. The graphics display at their actual size, so make them small enough to fit appropriately in the order form window.

Although you can customize the information included in the applet, you cannot change the interface, buttons, and the like. ■

People Directory

This database applet deserves a short chapter just to show you the power of database technology at Web sites, albeit in simple form. The trouble with putting a database applet in this book is that you need a database to use it. That puts it beyond the scope of the book—at least as far as providing the details and software to make it work for you. In this case, the database was created in Microsoft Access. The connection is via ODBC (Microsoft's standard database interface) to a Microsoft Internet Information server (a Web server). The program you download and use in your Web browser to access the database is a Java applet. This also can be set up for direct access to an Access database file through a Windows NT Web server via Java Database Connectivity (JBDC), the Java standard database interface. New in 1996, JDBC quickly is becoming widely used and incorporated into authoring tools; in other words, connecting these database applets to databases is becoming easier (for example, see Mojo at http://www.penumbrasoftware.com).

You can make the Web Contact applet (developed by Avitek of Boulder, Colorado, http://www.avitek.com) a directory of people at a company, an association, a Web site, or any other organization or group for which an online directory is appropriate. By inputting the name of a person (making a query), you can get basic information for that person such as address, phone number, and the like.

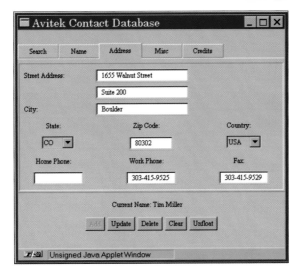

This by itself is a convenient service, but the applet also enables people to initiate their own listings in the directory by inputting information about themselves.

Thus, the applet receives data for the database as well as makes the data available via visitor queries. It's simple, straightforward, and handy. You can try this applet at Avitek's Web site along with its other useful database demos.

The CD-ROM does not include the applet for two reasons:

■ You would not be able to use it for your own database without engineering the proper connection with middleware or JDBC.

■ It will not run in your Web page using `codebase` to access the Avitek Web site because downloading an applet from one Web site to access a remote Web site is technically a security violation in the initial versions of Java. Both applet and server must be at the same Web site. Thus, Avitek does not allow access to its database from the Web Contact applet used at any Web site except `http://www.avitek.com`.

Why use Java to access a database when Web-database systems using CGI scripts work well? There are three primary reasons:

■ A Java applet presents a persistent interface with which visitors interact with the database. A Web server working through CGI scripts can generate a new Web page only in response to a query or data input.

■ The Java applet interface can be made to float (in other words, use a movable window), providing additional control and convenience to visitors.

■ User validation and input validation can be done by the applet, thereby taking some of the traffic load off the Web server.

For small databases, another reason is that the entire database (or a significant portion) can accompany the applet at the initial download. Thus, the Web server has no further traffic load after the initial download. Use this technique where narrow bandwidth is not a constraint. ■

Spreadsheets

Applet: spreadsheetname.class, SmartTable.zip

Visual Numerics, Inc. of Boulder, Colorado, (http://www.vni.com/products/wpd/ SmartTable/index.html) has done a great job with this spreadsheet authoring system. It makes applets that are precursors of the full-bodied Web programming that everyone will be using before long.

This applet works like the calculators (see "Calculator"). You can provide your visitors with embedded computing power for doing calculations of any kind. And it's easy to use, if you can use a spreadsheet program. Essentially, SmartTable takes a spreadsheet you have created using Microsoft Excel for Windows 5.0 or 7.0 and compiles it into a Java applet. The applet provides the full calculating power of the spreadsheet but does not reveal the underlying formulas.

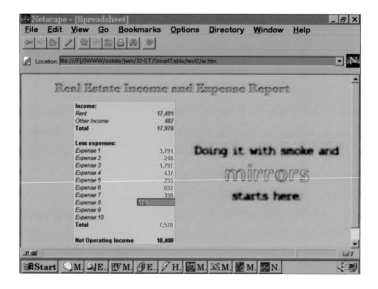

SmartTable provides a simple process for creating Web page spreadsheets:

1. Create the spreadsheet in Excel as you normally do.

2. Install the SmartTable program according to the instructions accompanying the trial version. The installation creates directories (folders) in which the SmartTable files are stored.

3. At a DOS prompt, use SmartTable.exe to compile the spreadsheet file spreadsheetname.xls. The text that follows simulates the command line.

```
C:\>smartt~1 bitbyte.xls
Visual Numerics SmartTableAlpha1 translator.
Copyright (C) Visual Numerics, Inc 1996. All rights reserved.
```

```
SmartTableAlpha1 expires after December 31, 1996.
javac bitbyte.java
<APPLET code=bitbyte width="343" height="154"></APPLET>
```

 In the DOS mode, Win95 abbreviates long file names to the 8.3 format. Thus, SmartTable.exe is expressed as smartt~1. The Excel file is bitbyte.xls. Notice that after SmartTable.exe translates the spreadsheet into Java code, it invokes the Java compiler javac.exe to compile the code into bitbyte.class. After compiling, SmartTable provides a *recommended* applet statement for the Web page including estimated dimensions. The estimated dimensions are probably not accurate, and you need to experiment with them (change them) to adjust them appropriately. The recommended applet statement is also incomplete, and you need to include the Archive attribute and CabBase parameter shown in the applet statement below.

4. Place the resulting applet in an HTML document. The minimum parameters for the applet can be simple. For the Archive attribute and CabBase parameter, be careful to plug in the correct paths to the required files.

```
<applet code="bitbyte" width="343" height="154"
Archive="../classes/SmartTable.zip">
<param name="CabBase" value="../classes/SmartTable.cab">
</applet>
```

5. Access the applet for testing on your computer with your browser.

6. When you have completed testing the applet on your computer, upload the HTML document, the applet (spreadsheetname.class), and the supporting SmartTable classes to your Web site. The best way to do this is to duplicate the directories (including files) on the Web site computer just as they were installed by SmartTable on your computer.

You can create a simple spreadsheet such as the example and turn it into a workable Java applet in less than an hour.

 For testing, keep Excel, the DOS prompt, your HTML editor, and your browser opened. Switch back and forth to test and revise. You probably have to close your browser and reopen it to make a fresh revision of the applet work.

SmartTable consists of a large number of files. You can think of it as a software authoring system that turns spreadsheets into applets. Unfortunately, it is not integrated into a GUI interface such as Jamba or Riada Cartel. Therefore, you must deal with a package of files and the DOS command line. In spite of the inconvenience, SmartTable is easy to use and works well. How amazing to be able to provide such functionality to your visitors in appropriate situations!

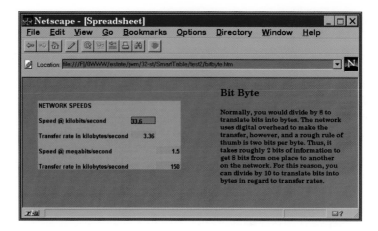

Additional parameters for SmartTable can be complex. This is a powerful program that provides much flexibility. (It even enables you to set parameters with JavaScript.) Keep in mind that SmartTable carries forward most of the formatting set in Excel such as cell color, font, text color, and so on. Thus, you can do most of your work in Excel where it's easy to do.

TIP Most spreadsheet programs export an Excel spreadsheet. Additionally, Excel imports most spreadsheets created in leading spreadsheet programs. Mac users can export an Excel for Mac spreadsheet, import it into Excel for Windows on a PC, and save it as an Excel for Windows spreadsheet. This general transferability makes it easy for you to get your spreadsheet in a form that SmartTable can use, even if you do not use Excel for Windows 5.0 or 7.0.

You can even publish a spreadsheet that fills an entire HTML document, leaving you little HTML work to do.

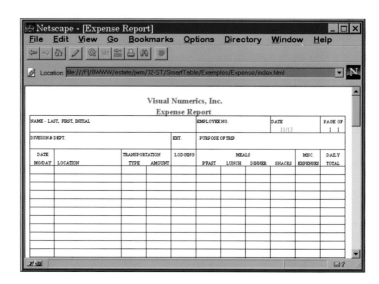

SmartTable compiles a spreadsheet with a graphic embedded in it. In the alpha version of the software, however, this feature worked awkwardly and presumably will be improved.

One way to look at spreadsheets within the context of Web publishing is that they can act as casual embedded programs; that is, they can be embedded in text to serve simple but specialized computing functions. Moreover, you can use them inconspicuously without fanfare. For information that includes calculations, this provides visitors with one of the great advantages of digital multimedia technology. ■

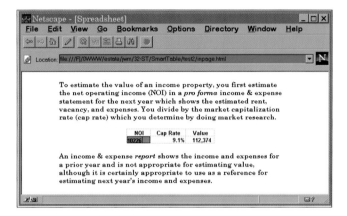

Office Applets

Fully-functioning Java applications delivered as applets over the Web (on both the Internet and on intranets) will become widespread before long. You can provide fully-functioning Java applets to your Web site visitors just as easily as any other applets. This means any type of program, regardless of size, potentially can be embedded in a Web page as a Java applet. This presents many exciting opportunities for marketing, customer service, online training, and publishing, to name a few.

What about providing word processors, spreadsheets, and other programs as a service for a fee? As people come online with network computers (NCs) and set-tops used with TVs, they will need to get all their programming from the Internet (or an intranet). The possibilities abound.

This chapter gives bread-and-butter examples of full-fledged Java applications delivered over the Web as Java applets: a word processor and a spreadsheet. Unfortunately, at the time this book went to press, it was a little premature to find finished products available in this category. Thus, there are none on the CD-ROM, but by the time you read this book, you will be able to obtain demonstration copies of a variety of full-fledged programs in the form of Java applets from the Web and try them out.

Word Processor

The well-tuned word processor and spreadsheet developed by Cooper & Peters of Boulder, Colorado (`http://www.cooper-peters.com`) are precursors of the many robust Java products soon to come.

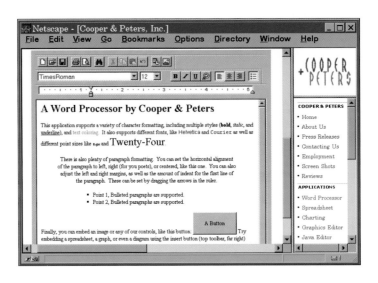

```
<applet code="CpWordProcessorDemo.class" archive="classes.zip" width="550"
height="500">
<param name="cabbase" value="classes.cab">
</applet>
```

Like almost every word processor, you click for a new document and start typing.

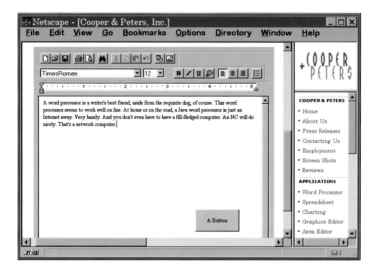

The essential question is not will a word processor work online, but how well does it respond—that is, does it feel quick and snappy like a desktop word processor? This depends on a number of things:

- **Current Server Traffic.** If traffic is heavy, response time may be slow.

- **Bandwidth.** A narrow bandwidth for the client connection to the Web or the server connection to the Web (for example, under 56Kb per second) slows the response time.

- **Poorly Programmed Applet.** A word processor not programmed properly may slow the response time. Initially, Java word processor applets will be imperfect.

- **Poorly Balanced Program.** A developer must decide how much of the applet processing to retain on the server, and how much to relegate to the client. An improper balance may slow the overall response time.

The ideal, of course, is a response time comparable to a desktop program. Such response times are achievable but may not be always available. Occasional slowdowns can occur.

As for features, it takes a huge Java applet to equal the features of a typical desktop word processor. Initially, at least, Java word processor applets will be thin cousins of the real thing. Power users may not want to use a Java word processor applet. For many purposes, however, these applets will be adequate. This is especially true where you provide word processors to Web site visitors for a specific and limited purpose or as a temporary convenience.

You can see by the previous `applet` statement that the markups to install a word processor do not have to be complex. However, the system of Java classes stored on the server is likely to be more robust than a simple applet. In fact, if a portion of the applet processing is to be done on the server computer, then that part of the applet becomes a word processor server. This presents all the normal considerations regarding installing server software on the server computer.

Spreadsheet

Cooper & Peters also offers a spreadsheet program applet. It works much like a desktop spreadsheet and is easy to use.

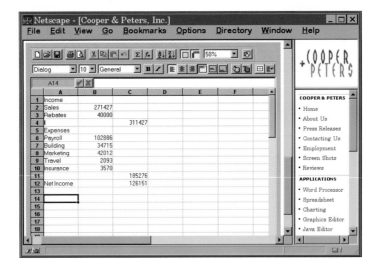

```
<applet code="CpSpreadsheetDemo.class" archive="classes.zip"
width="585" height="500">
<param name="cabbase" value="classes.cab">
</applet>
```

Again, special purposes and convenience are some of the reasons to provide this functionality to Web site visitors where appropriate.

TIP The difference between the Cooper & Peters spreadsheet applet and the Smart Tables applet (covered in the previous chapter) is the difference between full functionality and finished product. The Cooper & Peters applet provides visitors the capability to create any type of spreadsheet. Smart Tables applets are financial models or databases that have been programmed already and cannot be altered. Thus, the Cooper & Peters spreadsheet does not necessarily compete with Smart Tables applets.

The use of full-fledged applications in a Java applet format will not be limited to word processors and spreadsheets. Before long many familiar desktop programs will become available in applet format and people will use them online through their Web browsers.

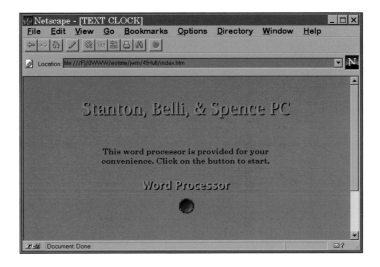

Applix Anyware Suite

The Applix Anyware office suite of Java programs includes a word processor, spreadsheet, and the specialized supporting server software as well as other programs. Applix of Westboro, Massachusetts (http://www.applix.com) has years of experience providing business programs online. Applix now has ported its online software to Java to be the first to market with robust and fully-functional office software. Applix Anyware starts with a button.

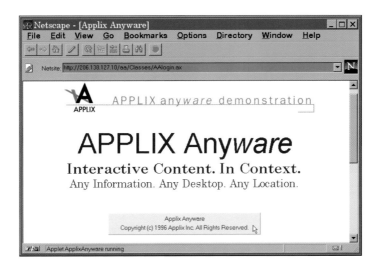

```
<applet codebase="/aa/Classes/" code="ApplixAnyware.class"
width="350" height="50" ARCHIVE="anyware.zip">
<param name="port" value="start">
<param name="host" value="espresso.applix.com">
<param name="uri" value="AA.ax?">
<param name="tid" value="2764">
<param name="browser" value="Mozilla/3.0Gold (Win95; I)">
<param name="helpURI" value="/aa/Help">
<param name="noDelay" value="0">
<!-- WEBSHEET -->
<param name="fgColor" value="#000040">
<param name="bgColor" value="#DDDDDD">
<param name="EndingURL" value="http://espresso.applix.com/Demo/
DemoThanks.html">
<param name="EndingURLTarget" value="_top">
</applet>
```

You start the Applix WebSheet by selecting the file you want.

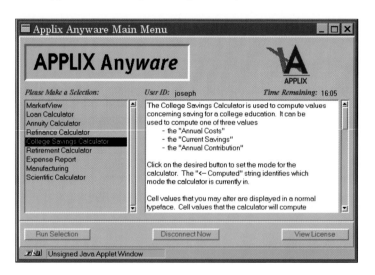

The spreadsheet looks and works like other spreadsheets, except that you must store your work on the server computer.

The Applix word processor works similarly and also stores its document files on the server computer. As with other Java word processors, spreadsheets, and chat programs, Applix Anyware requires a server to be run on the server computer.

Providing Office Applets

Here are some things to remember when you provide robust Java applets:

■ If an applet's file size is large, give visitors an option to invoke it. This can be done two ways. First, you can provide a warning and a special hyperlink to a separate Web page where the application automatically downloads. Or, you can use a warning and a Java applet button that downloads the Java application when the button is clicked. The second choice requires a separate button applet.

■ Make sure that the licensing agreement for the application covers your intended use. If you go public on the Internet with a licensing violation, you may get a nasty letter from an attorney, or worse.

■ If you don't want everyone to use the Java application, put it behind a password gateway or use some other restrictive device.

■ Network computer (NC) users will be prime candidates to use such Java applications. NCs have no permanent memory and you will have to provide hard disk storage for such visitors to store their work in progress (if appropriate for the particular applet you offer). Keep in mind that set-top boxes are NCs that use a TV instead of a computer monitor for display. Some TVs sold in 1997 will have set-top boxes (NCs) built-in. The use of set-top boxes and NCs will increase in 1997 and thereafter. ■

133

AppletAce: Introduction

Macromedia has developed a number of spiffy little applets you can add to a Web page, and has bundled them in a user-friendly construction kit called AppletAce. Ace and the applets, which can be used to make banners, bullets, charts and imagemaps (see the following chapters), are currently available as a free package at the Macromedia Web site (http://www.macromedia.com/software/powerapplets/).

Ace offers you a series of tabs, panels, and text boxes for data input and then outputs the code into a text window where you copy it to paste into an HTML document. You can create most of the applets manually and some HTML tweaking if you choose.

Macromedia plans to market this package in 1997, but as of this writing Ace is an unsupported beta product. You may find it easy to configure the Banner and Bullet applets by hand, but the Imagemap and Charts applets are much easier with Ace. At this point, you cannot reopen a finished applet to make changes, nor can you change the HTML output manually within Ace. Documentation for most features is plentiful on the Macromedia site, if inconsistently organized.

The applet's intent is to make configuring easier, saving you time and effort, and the fully realized product will probably do so. As you set the parameters for your applet, you can flip to a preview page to see its appearance and behavior. If you make a syntax error, you get an error message. Ace includes a library of class files, from which it make copies of the files you need and puts them in the directory you specify.

When you have finished configuring your applet, copy the code from the HTML screen and paste it into your HTML document. It's a straight copy-and paste-operation for PC owners. Macintosh owners must first save the code as a document, then open it in a text or HTML editor. You cannot make parameter changes in the Ace HTML window but can add, modify, and delete parameters after you paste it into your HTML document.

When you first open Ace you see a tab where you choose which type of applet you want to create. This also is where you set the general parameters such as width, height, alignment, and where you enter the path to the directory where you want to place your HTML document and class files. You also can use a Browse button to find the directory. Once you select the kind of applet you want to build, Ace presents you with a series of new tabs specific to your choice.

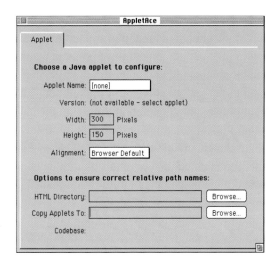

In subsequent chapters we will tell you more about the four applets that come with Ace. ■

135

AppletAce: Banners

The Banners applet displays a series of moving messages that you can wrap in a frame and display over a colored background or a background image. You can choose the font, size, style, and color of the text, and the speed and style of the animation. You can designate both an entrance and exit effect for each message: scrolling up or down, right or left, or zooming in or out. You even can pick a "squeeze" effect for the frame and background.

To configure a Banners applet with Ace, go to the Applet panel and select Banners on the the Applet Name list. Five new tabs appear at the top of the screen: Text, Animation, Background, Preview, and HTML.

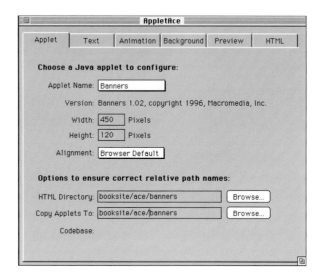

The Text panel is where you enter the text you want to display onscreen and determine how it will look. You can create a series of messages that play in sequence, each with its own style. For each message, you can set the color of the text and the name and style of the font, including emboss or shadow effects. The first line establishes default settings for the text. Set new values for any subsequent line you want to change. You also must set new background and animation values for every line you want to change. One of the color options is color cycling. If you want one message broken into two or more lines, use the character \n as a "new line" character at the point where you want to divide the message.

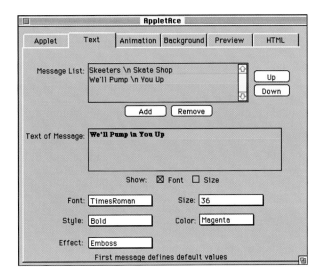

The Banners Animation panel is where you specify the animation sequence for each message and the background. In addition to beginning and ending effects, you can specify a pause length and other timing variables. The speed of movement is based on two factors: how many steps the message is moved every second, and how far it is moved each step.

Specify the number of steps or "frames" per second (which show up in the output parameters as fps) and the number of pixels the message moves every frame. This is called "cpf" (Change Per Frame), and is limited by the speed of the user's computer. The Alignment menu enables you to set five possible "stop" points for each message—where the text is placed after it finishes its entrance move. A repeat value can be set for each line in a message list. It controls the number of times the message will be displayed before moving on to the next message.

AppletAce

| Applet | Text | Animation | Background | Preview | HTML |

Animation for: `We'll Pump \n You Up`

Entrance: `zoomIn`   Frames Per Second: `30`

Pause: `1` seconds   Change Per Frame: `4`

Exit: `zoomOut`   Repeat: `0` times

Alignment: `Top`

The Background panel enables you to set the background style, which can be a solid color or a GIF or JPEG image, and is customizable for each message. This is also where you set entrance and exit transitions for the background and create borders. Your choices for Bg Entrance are appear (which translates in the HTML output as BgEnter=none) and zoomIn (which translates as BgEnter=squeeze). Your Bg Exit choices include disappear (which translates as BgExit=none) and zoomOut (BgExit=squeeze). More on this later. You also can specify a URL and even target a frame for each message. Use the pull-down menus to choose background and border colors. You can select a predefined color, or choose hex, in which case you will enter a hex value in the text field next to the menu.

AppletAce

| Applet | Text | Animation | Background | Preview | HTML |

Background for: `We'll Pump \n You Up`

Background: ○ Solid Color: `Default`

● Tiled Image: `images/SKATES.GIF` [Browse...]

Bg Entrance: ● Appear   ○ Zoom In

Bg Exit: ○ Disappear   ● Zoom Out

URL when Clicked:

Netscape Frame: _____ (optional)

Border Width: _____ (border applies to all messages)

Border Color: `Default`

You can test your parameter settings at any time by clicking the Preview tab.

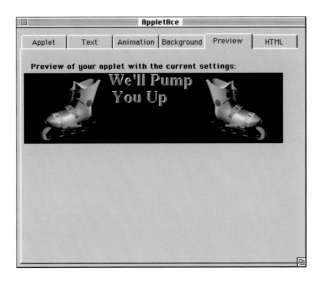

When you have finished, you can save and copy the code from the HTML screen so that you can paste it into your HTML document. Remember that Macintosh owners must first save the code as a document, then open it in a text or HTML editor. Remember too that you cannot change the parameters in Ace's HTML window, but can make changes after pasting the code into your HTML document.

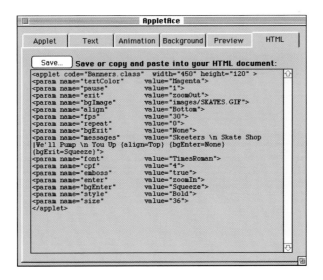

As you review the HTML output, note the value `squeeze` for the `bgEnter` parameter. This is set on the background panel as `zoomIn` and `zoomOut`, and affects the border as well as its contents. A squeeze exit for one message followed by a squeeze entrance for the next one makes a particularly effective transition. Background transitions operate independently of the foreground transitions, which are set on the animation panel, and include a wide range of wipes, scrolling, and color cycling options.

With or without Ace, Banners is a versatile applet with many useful features and a long list of parameters that you can use to customize your site. A complete list of the parameters is available on the Macromedia site and on the CD-ROM in the back of this book. ■

AppletAce: Bullets

Macromedia's Bullets applet lets you animate bullets and lines (which the applet calls "separators") with cycling color patterns that you can configure in a variety of ways. You can pick the range of colors and specify the speed, smoothness, pauses, and background color. The rectangular and circular objects you define can be any size, and you can create some interesting and unusual effects on your pages by playing with the parameters and creating patterns of repeating applets.

The Bullets applet is fairly simple to configure in the Ace applet builder. At the top of the screen are tabs labeled Applet, Bullet, Preview, and HTML.

Set the dimensions of the object you are working on the Applet panel. On the Bullet panel, select either a separator or bullet by clicking the Rectangle or Ellipse radio button. Next specify the dimensions of the object you are creating, and set the direction and movement of the color cycling.

Your choices for Transitions include:

- Fade In: colors cycle from the edges into the center.
- Fade Out: colors cycle from the center out to the edges.
- Fade Left: colors cycle from right to left.
- Fade Right: colors cycle from left to right.
- Fade Up: colors cycle from the bottom to the top.
- Fade Down: colors cycle from the top to the bottom.
- Fade: entire bullet fades from one color to the next.

On the same panel are Speed and Smoothness controls that determine the overall speed of motion. The speed parameter controls how many times per second the animation updates (subject to the speed of the system on which the applet is running). Smoothness indicates how far the colors shift each step of the animation. A smaller value causes a smoother animation, but the animation runs slower. Larger steps result in coarser but faster movements.

The Blend Colors option produces smoother color transitions with intermediate colors. Specify the number of colors you want to display simultaneously and set a background color. For color selections you can use the assigned color palette or provide a hex value. You also can change the order of the colors and add new ones. You can also specify a pause between colors. Check the Preview panel as you make changes to see the results.

When you are satisfied, you can copy the code generated by the program from the HTML panel and paste it into your document. Ace copies the class files you need and puts them where you want them, typically in the same directory as the HTML document. You can do additional tweaking of the parameters at this point, as you would with any other applet. A complete list of the parameters that work with this applet is available at the Macromedia Web site and on the CD-ROM in the back of this book.

The following code describes a simple bar-shaped separator that fades up from a black background to a green bar and then fades back to black. The fadeAmount parameter determines how fast the applet fades from one color to the next. Lower values make more intermediate colors. The rate of color change is established by the fps (frames per second) value, with the upper limits dependent upon the speed of the user's computer. The displayColors setting indicates the number of colors that display onscreen at any given time. The colors value establishes the range of the colors cycled. In this example there are only two settings: hex numbers representing a particular shade of green, and a basic black.

```
<applet code="Bullets.class" width="551" height="4">
<param name="effect" value="fadeout">
<param name="fadeAmount" value="15">
<param name="displayColors" value="20">
<param name="fps" value="10">
<param name="bgColor" value="#000000">
<param name="style" value="separator">
<param name="colors" value="#009865, #000000">
</applet>
```

Note that the parameters as listed in the HTML output often use a slightly different terminology from that on the panel where they are set. On the Bullet panel, the fadeAmount parameter is set by the Blend Colors field, the displayColors setting is established by the Number of Colors field, and the fps value is set by the Speed field. Also on the same panel: Set the value for bgColor with the Background Color field. (#000000 is the hex number for black.) The style parameter is set by the Shape field. Separator is the term used for a rectangle or line. Set the colors for the object you are creating in the Colors field. (#009865 is a shade of green.)

A simple button on the same page that uses the same color and cycling parameters attracts attention without screaming at the viewer. The only changes here are the style setting, which is for a button (called an ellipse on the bullet panel) instead of separator (or rectangle), and the dimensions of the applet. Bullet is the default with this applet, so we have only to omit the style parameter and adjust the dimensions.

```
<applet code="Bullets.class" width="13" height="13">
```

Used together in repetitions, the two applets add a stylish look to a Web page.

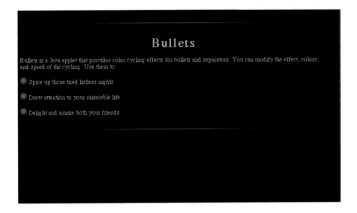

You can create a variety of effects on a Web page by changing the size, shape, and parameters of your applet. Experiment to find designs that you like. Repeatedly pasting the applet over and over into your document can create some interesting and unusual patterns. Using an HTML authoring program that recognizes applets can make this process much easier. ■

AppletAce: Imagemaps

Use the Imagemap applet from Macromedia to define and highlight hot spots on a graphic of your choice, making the hot spots into button objects and linking them to specified URLs. You can assign a text window that pops up to give the user additional information, and replacement images that appear when the mouse enters (rolls over) the selected area or clicks it. This image by Kate Reed of Luong Tam Designs illustrates how it works.

When you configure an Imagemap applet using AppletAce, you work with six tabs at the top of the screen: Applet, Hot Areas, Effects, General, Preview, and HTML.

The applet panel is where you designate the object's dimensions and establish directory paths. You can create a fully functional imagemap by using just the Hot Areas panel. Use the Effects and General tabs to customize the pop-up text window and to define and position any replacement images.

The first step (after when you activate AppletAce) is to load the base image via the Hot Areas panel. Locate the image file with the browser box. Any JPEG or GIF image works on the Mac. Currently the Windows version supports only GIF images.

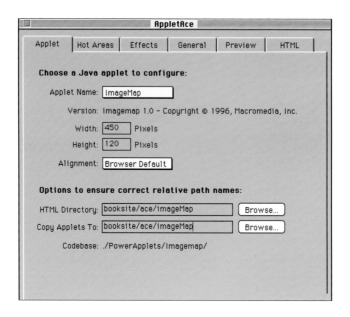

Use the two pull-down lists on the Hot Areas panel to establish what effects you want to occur when someone moves the mouse over the image or clicks it. For each of these two actions you choose among the following:

- none: no action occurs.

- invert: all the colors in the hot area are inverted (much like a film negative).

- outline: an outline of the hot area is drawn.

- replaceImage: the hot area is replaced with the rectangular portion of another image.

You may notice that when outline is selected, a color selection list appears to the right. Use this list to specify the desired color of the outline, working with the assigned colors or adding a hex number.

To specify the replacement image, go to the General tab panel and use the file browser box to find the image you want to use. The applet replaces the specified coordinates of the hot area with the same region in the replacement image. Use the mouse to drag out the new area.

A toolbox on the Hot Areas panel with four tools enables you to select and define rectangular, circular, and irregular-shaped areas on your image as hotspots. If you make a mistake, just select an area and delete it using the delete/backspace key.

There is also an input box where you enter text that you want to pop up for each button when the user holds the mouse pointer over the hot area for a few seconds. Switch back to the General tab to define the text attributes and background color for the pop-up text.

Below the text input box on the Hot Areas tab is another box where you enter the URL that you want linked to the hotspot. You also can target a Netscape frame where you want the page to appear.

The Effects panel provides an alternative way to configure up to two effects for each hot area, one for Mouse Enter and one for Mouse Down. It is also where you establish replacement images—if you have chosen that option and set the coordinates. Your cursor becomes a rectangular tool used to outline the section of the replacement image that you want to use.

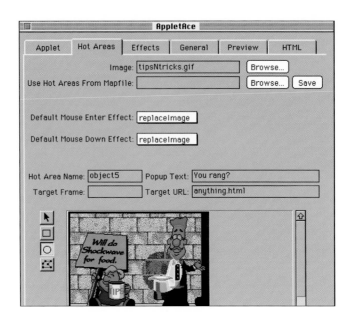

When your selection is highlighted, it appears on the main image where you can position it more precisely by clicking and dragging it to the desired location.

On the left, there is a text field that displays the coordinates of the mouse cursor within each of the images. Use this for precise guidelines when selecting or positioning a replacement.

In addition to replacement images, you can specify the background color and pop-up text options on the Imagemap General panel. The background color setting is used when you have a GIF image with a transparency to establish the color that shows through.

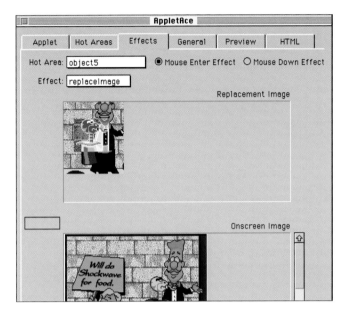

You can flip back and forth to the Preview panel as you change the parameters to see the final effect.

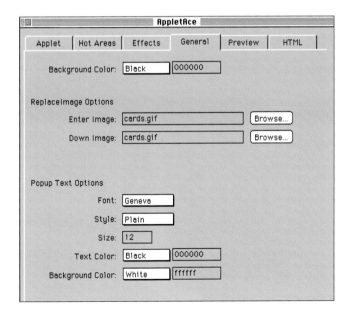

When you have finished, output the code to your HTML document by copying and pasting. You can, of course, continue to make changes in the applet's parameters after inserting it in your document. A complete list of parameters is available on the Macromedia Web site or on the CD-ROM in the back of this book.

An imagemap for a job site uses the following code. Clicking on the magician's hat results in a snake sticking his head up and triggers a link to the current job list.

```
<applet code="ImageMap.class" width="234" height="268">
<param name="image" value="tipsNtricks.gif">
<param name="defaultDownEffect" value="replaceImage,down">
<param name="defaultEnterEffect" value="replaceImage,enter">
<param name="area2"
value="object5,circle,jobs.html,null,155,97,188,130,replaceImage,enter
¦17¦27¦57¦53¦129¦69,replaceImage,down¦16¦16¦48¦64¦130¦65">
<param name="area1"
value="object3,circle,null,null,341,61,341,61,null,null,replaceImage,d
own¦341¦61¦0¦0¦341¦61">
<param name="toolTips" value="object5¦You rang?">
<param name="enterImage value="snake3.gif">
<param name="bgColor" value="Black">
<param name="tipbgcolor" value="White">
<param name="tipfont" value="Geneva">
<param name="tipsize" value="12">
<param name="tipstyle" value="Plain">
<param name="tipcolor" value="Black">
<param name="downImage" value="snake2.gif">
</applet>
```

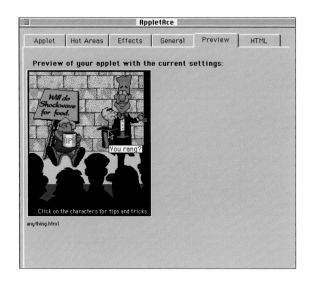

The parameter `area2` defines the image area we have turned into a hot spot. object5 is the name of the button we have created. It's a circle and is linked to a document called job.html. The parameter `toolTips` shows the accompanying mouse-activated pop-up text. Note that snake3.gif is the name of the replacement image the user sees upon moving the cursor over the hotspot, and that snake2.gif is the image activated when the user clicks the mouse. ■

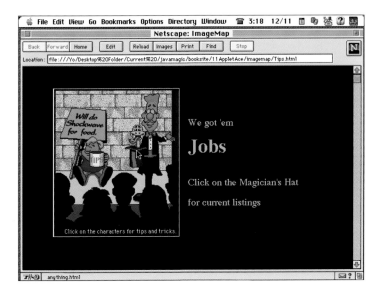

AppletAce: Charts

Macromedia's Charts applet enables you to create a bar chart on your Web page using one of four different chart formats. You set the format, colors, and spacing of the bars, title displays, and border styles. Data for a chart is imported from a text file you designate and loaded dynamically each time the chart displays. You also can specify an interval at which the data reloads.

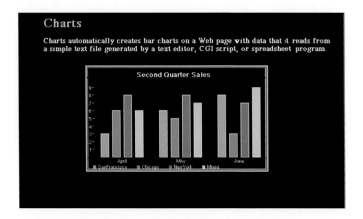

To create a chart using AppletAce, select Charts on the opening panel, after which you see four new tabs at the top of the window: Chart Style, Colors, Preview, and HTML.

Use the Chart Style panel to set the general appearance and layout of the chart. This is also where you select the data file on which the chart is based. You specify the name of this file and its path or simply select it with the Browse button.

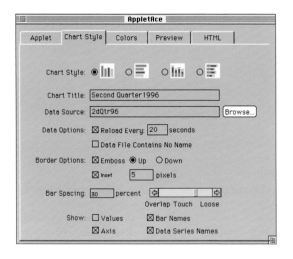

The data file used here as an example is a simple text file created in a word processing program that was given the name 2dQtr96. It includes sales figures for four different cities for the months of April, May, and June. Here's the data in the document:

```
"Second Quarter Sales" April May June
SanFrancisco 3 6 8
Chicago 6 5 3
NewYork 8 8 7
Miami 6 7 9
```

The example shown uses a vbar or vertical staggered Chart Style, one of four styles that you can select. Just click the radio button next to the icon that represents the chart style you want to use. The other choices are horizontal staggered, vertical stacked, and horizontal stacked.

Staggered bars are displayed side-by-side. In a stacked chart the bars are laying on top of one another. To see how your data looks with different chart styles, click each style and then go to the Preview panel.

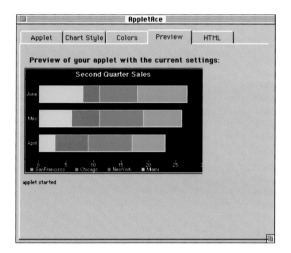

153

Your data can stand apart, overlap, or abut—depending on how you set the Bar Spacing parameter on the Chart Style tab. You also can give your chart a title that appears at the top when it is displayed. Keep in mind, however, that this title will be overridden by any title that you provide in a data file.

With the Data Options on this panel you can instruct the applet to reload the chart from the data file at given intervals. This allows for dynamic updating from a CGI script or other source. The Data File Contains No Names option is explained later in this chapter.

The Border Options enable you to customize the appearance of the borders. Emboss results with a 3-D look. You specify whether the embossing is to be Up or Down by clicking the appropriate button. The Inset option controls the spacing between the border and the applet.

Bar Spacing enables you to set the amount of relative space between the bars. The default is zero, which means the bars in a cluster just touch one another. A negative value makes the bars overlap and a positive value causes the bars to have more space between them. You can use the slider to set the spacing or enter a value in the text field.

Four checkboxes at the bottom of the Chart Style panel let you turn chart labels on or off. Values are the numbers that the bars represent. The Bar Names are the labels for each set of data. The Axis is the number axis along the side or top. Data Series Names is the label for each of the series of data.

In our example, Values is not checked. Checking it would give us a number at the top of each bar. The Bar Names include the months of April, May, and June, and the Data Series Names are the names of the cities charted. You can see the results in the preview panel.

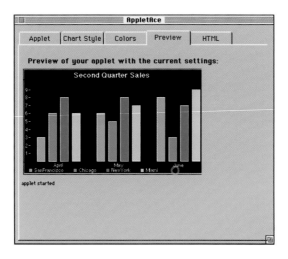

Switch to the Colors panel to set the color for each item in the chart. You can specify colors for the chart outline, text, border, background, and shadow. You also can specify the color for each series, using an assigned color or a hex number.

The data for your bar chart is stored in a text file, which may be generated in a text editor or a spreadsheet program like Microsoft Excel (using the Save as text option). This allows the data to be modified and updated dynamically at specific intervals via a CGI script.

When creating your data file, place each data series on a separate line. You are allowed six lines. Each line should contain the same number of values separated by spaces or tabs.

Unless the Data File Contains No Names box is checked, it is assumed that the file contains title data, and is stored in the form:

```
title_override val1name val2name val3name
series1name ser1val1 ser1val2 ser1val3
series2name ser2val1 ser2val2 ser2val3
```

Here title override replaces the title given in the Chart Title field on the Chart Style panel. If you *don't* want to override that title, you replace the name represented by title override with a null string that consists of a pair of empty quotes. It looks like this: " ".

The labels for each value follow the title on the same line. This is followed by up to six lines that include a data series name followed by the data values. Any of these names may be omitted by entering a null string: " ". If a name contains any spaces, it must be enclosed in quotation marks. Either single or double quotes may be used. If the name contains a single quote, it can be enclosed in double quotes and vice versa.

If you want to display data that contain only numbers and no names, you can check the Data File Contains No Names box on the Chart Style panel. In that event the data in the file should take the form:

```
series1val1  series1val2  series1val3
series2val1  series2val2  series2val3
```

When your bar chart looks the way you want it, open the HTML panel, copy the code generated by Ace, and paste it into your HTML document.

The complete code for the applet shown in this chapter looks like this:

```
<applet code="Charts.class" width="350" height="200">
<param name="url" value="2dQtr96">
<param name="barspace" value="30">
<param name="inset" value="5">
<param name="title" value="Second Quarter 1996">
<param name="type" value="vbar">
<param name="options" value="showAxis,showBarNames,showSeriesNames,
embossUp">
<param name="reloadInterval" value="10">
<param name="colors" value="Cyan,Green,Red,Yellow">
<param name="bgColor" value="Black">
<param name="borderColor" value="Black">
<param name="outlineColor" value="White">
<param name="textColor" value="White">
</applet>
```

You can continue to change the appearance of your bar chart by modifying the parameters after you paste them into your HTML document. Changing vbar to hbar in our example would result in horizontal bars instead of vertical bars. Changing our colors would result in a chart that looks completely different. ■

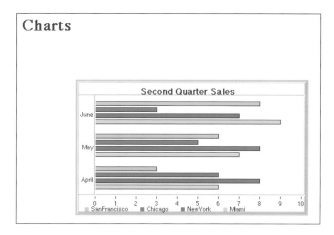

Riada Cartel: Running Marquee

Applet: Cartel.class

Looking for versatile, attractive, dynamic, and easy-to-use applets? Riada Cartel's marquee applets fit that description well. Riada Cartel sells for about $30, but the developer Daniel Adair Riada, of Melbourne, Australia (http://www.riada.com.au), offers a lower price for those willing to link his or her Web site to Riada's. Consider this software something of a Windows 95 authoring program; it makes spiffy marquees for you, and more.

Install this applet like you would any other program. It comes with examples and tutorials. But don't flinch. Cartel is easy to use. It has a Wizard that does it all for you. You can download this program, install it, make your first banner, and publish the banner to your Web site—all in less than 30 minutes. You need to purchase a registration number, however, in order to enable the program to publish the banner.

Using the Wizard's second screen, you can investigate the characteristics of the banner lights as a first step.

The first variation is Fast, a small light that enables a faster moving banner. Select variations by clicking on the appropriate radio button.

The second variation is LED, which emits a glow effect.

The last variation is LCD, which has larger lights than Fast.

Next, you can change the size of the banner by changing the number of pixels for its dimensions. At the Edit menu select Rio Properties and then Size.

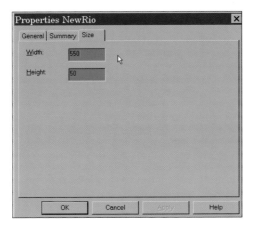

You can change the font using the Wizard (first screen and fourth screen). You have three choices: sans serif (default), wide, and serif.

You type the words for your banner right in the Wizard (fourth screen). Unfortunately, you cannot paste text into the Wizard, although apparently you can type as much text as you desire.

159

TIP **Because the text loops in the scroll effect, leave a space at the end of your text. Also, place a space at the beginning of your text, or it may abut the frame in a distracting way for some effects.**

To easily change the colors of the text, highlight the text you want to change and make a selection from the color menu. You can change all the text or one word of the text.

You even can create a rainbow effect for a static banner using rainbow in the Wizard's effect selection (fourth screen).

The Wizard makes changing the background easy too. There are two parts:

- ■ The light off color. Make it dark gray (40,40,40) for traditional banners.
- ■ The color behind the lights. Make it black (0,0,0) for traditional banners.

By clicking on the color sample, you bring up the Windows 95 color window.

For special effects, however, you can make the two background colors the same (gray, for example) or noticeably different (green and gray).

You can even get ultra creative (red and purple).

The Wizard enables you to change the effect too. The default is scroll left. The text enters on the right and moves toward the left. The fresh marquee trails the existing marquee text.

Among the many effect choices are swipe (left), which moves fresh text over the existing text, and reveal (right), which reveals the fresh text behind an invisible moving, vertical line.

Some of the choices, such as show, produce static text.

The clever Wizard also allows you to change the color and shape of the border with a selection of controls on the third screen. You can make the border any color, such as blue with a beveled look, orange with a groove look, or rose with a rounded look.

You can make the banner larger, the border the same color as the Web page background, the border width one pixel, the light off and light background colors the same colors as the Web page; this gives the effect of the banner being right in the Web page itself.

Riada Cartel provides attractive and useful marquee graphics. Think of practical ways to use them. Observe how others use them. They can be a real workhorse for you. Fortunately, Cartel is remarkably easy to use to create the examples described above. But it does more, too, and some of the advanced capabilities are demonstrated in the next chapter.

Under the Generate menu, you can select Publish to create an HTML page and publish your Riada marquee applets complete with all necessary classes. To revise an applet, simply use the Wizard to tinker with it and then republish. ■

Riada Cartel: Action Marquee

Applet: Cartel.class

As promised in the previous chapter, with Riada Cartel the folks in Melbourne bring you advanced marquee techniques. Because Riada Cartel is a marquee authoring program, it works similarly to a Java authoring program, but with capability limited to creating marquees. In this chapter, the marquee presentation contains a series of marquees integrated into a Web page between two graphics that acts as a hyperlink.

Text	Color	Scroll Action
Welcome!	Yellow	Scroll down [Pause about 4000]
The time is {Time(1)}	Magenta	Scroll down [Pause about 5000]
Have a nice {Day()}.	Cyan	Scroll left [Pause about 5000]
Visit the BookCenter. Click here now.	Orange	Scroll left [Pause about 1000]

How does it work? The first text ("Welcome!") scrolls down, followed by a four-second pause.

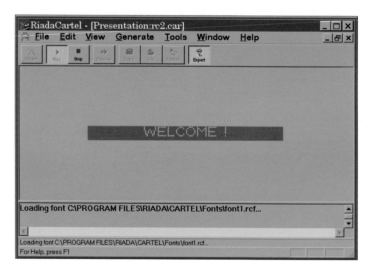

Then the text "The time is {Time(1)}" scrolls down, followed by a five-second pause. In this case, the time expression Time( ) is embedded between braces { }.

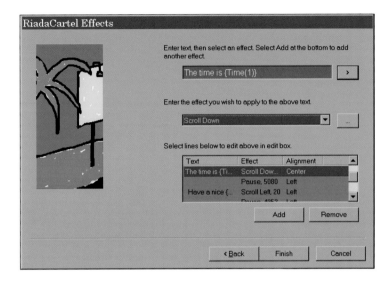

When displayed, it shows the time (obtained from the computer clock).

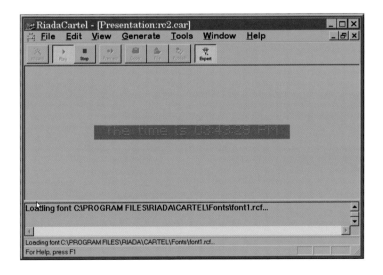

Next, the text "Have a nice {Day()}" scrolls in to the left, followed by a five-second pause. Again, the day expression is embedded between braces. When displayed, it shows the day.

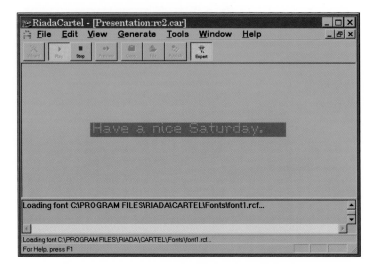

Finally, the text "Visit the BookCenter. Click here now." scrolls in to the left, followed by a one-second pause after which the cycle repeats itself.

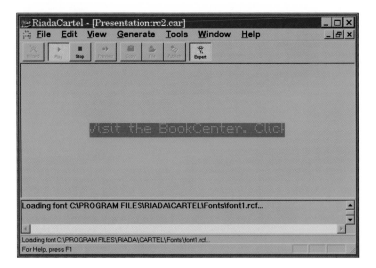

On the Web page, the applet is between two graphics; the background color, the Off color, and the border color are all green to match the Web page background. Set the border thickness at one pixel. Use the third screen of the Wizard to make these settings.

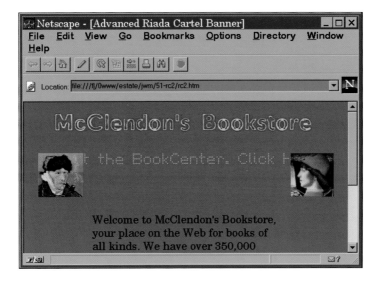

The `applet` statement is complex, but that's of little concern. Riada Cartel automatically generates the applet statement in an Web page. You only need to put it into your own Web page by copying and pasting.

```
<applet code="Cartel.class" width="420" height="40">
<param name="name" value="NewRio">
<param name="Reg1" value="7GQWGA001">
<param name="Reg2" value="W3ZAKLVN1">
<param name="Audio" value="laser.au">
<param name="Fonts" value="font1.rcf">
<param name="PageEnter" value=";0|80~119~0~2~15~1|92~0~119~0|:0~119~0|7
[Center][Yellow] WELCOME ! [ScrollUp][Left][Pause,4185][Center][Magenta]
The time is {N2_1_3}[ScrollDown][Left][Pause,5080][Cyan]  Have a nice
{K23}. [ScrollLeft][Pause,4952][Orange]  Visit the BookCenter. Click here
now. [ScrollLeft][Pause]~0">
<param name="PageExit" VALUE=".">
<param name="MouseUp" value="&http://www.bookcenter.com~_self|+0~0~0">
</applet>
```

Under the Generate menu, select Publish to generate your Riada marquee applet complete with all necessary classes.

165

You can easily place graphics on the left and right sides of the applet.

```
<img src="left.jpg"><applet>[applet statement from above]
</applet><img src="right.jpg">
```

Other than adding embedded expressions, creating this applet is much the same as in the previous chapter on Riada Cartel. You can use the advanced capability of Riada Cartel, however, to create other functionality. In this case, a mouse click while the cursor is over the banner transfers the visitor to another URL. You go into the Design mode (View, Design) to set this up. When you first go into the Design mode, it is set to the PageEnter event.

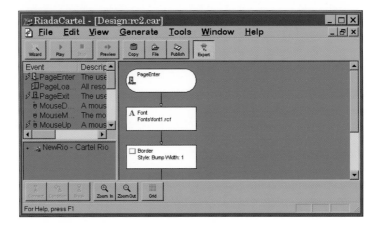

You want to change to the MouseUp event by clicking MouseUp under Event.

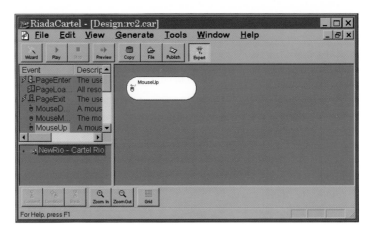

Then attach an action to the MouseUp event. Expand New Rio. In this instance, you drag and drop Internet-Jump to the MouseUp event, which automatically brings up a window where you add the Jump to URL on the Internet Action. Click OK and it automatically connects to the MouseUp event.

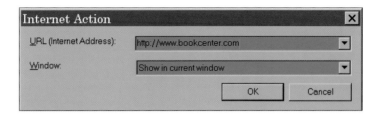

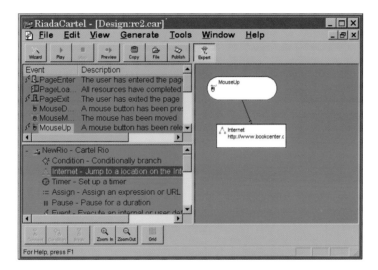

Also, give this action a sound by repeating the same steps above but using the Audio-Start action. Remember, Java handles only .au audio files. After highlighting both the Jump to and Audio actions with the Ctrl key depressed, click the Connect button.

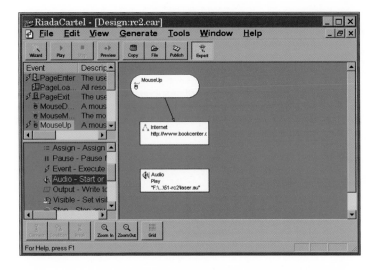

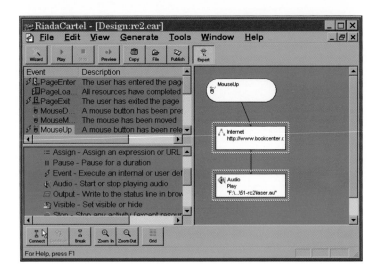

When the cursor passes over the applet and the visitor clicks, the applet transfer the visitor to the specified URL, while at the same time playing the audio file.

Again, under the Generate menu, select Publish to generate your Riada marquee applet in any directory or on the Internet complete with all necessary classes.

Riada Cartel offers lots of other multimedia programming actions such as Condition (conditional branching), Event (execute an event), Pause, Assign (assign content to a variable), Visible (true or false), Output (write to status line), Stop, and additional actions that change the way the marquees are displayed. Try some. ■

Egor: Animation

Egor from Sausage Software of Doncaster, Victoria, Australia, (http://www.sausage.com) is a Java animation authoring program for Windows available at retail stores. It enables you to make versatile animation applets easily. It does everything but the artwork for you. As with all animation, the artwork is crucial. This chapter features Sausage's cartoon character named Egor. The authoring program comes with five cartoon drawings (GIFs) of Egor as well as a handful of other cartoon drawings with which you can experiment.

As you can see, flashed in sequence these images show an animated cartoon. It's easy to create such an animation with Egor. You open a new file and select the Frames tab, then add graphic files sequentially by clicking on the Add button and specifying a file. It's that simple. If you want to get rid of a image in the sequence, simply drag it to the guillotine. Delightful. You also can convert images into an appropriate format or play the images in sequence for a rough animation preview.

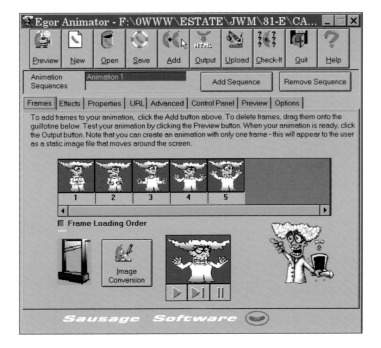

Use the Effects tab for making refinements. You can set the timing and a time limit.

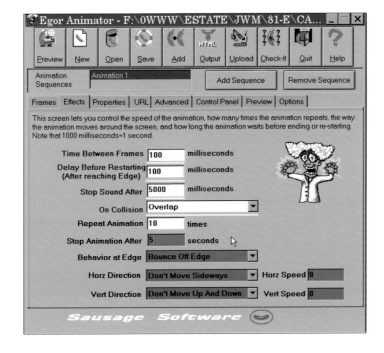

Other tabs provide further creative controls (setting the background color for the applet). You can incorporate audio files, create hyperlinks, set backgrounds, and even make your animation sprite move around the screen.

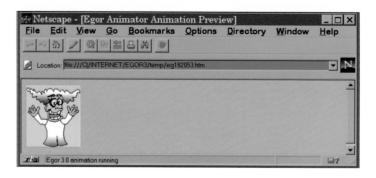

By clicking the Upload button, Egor automatically installs the applet in a Web page for you, even on the Internet, where you can preview it using a Web browser.

```
<applet code="anim3simple.class" width="117" height="128">
<param name="name" value="egor" >
<param name="num_sprites" value="1">
<param name="priority" value="0">
<param name="rollover" value="false">
<param name="pause" value="100">
```

```
<param name="enddelay" value="100">
<param name="soundtime" value="5000">
<param name="on_collision" value="overlap">
<param name="bg" value="255,255,10">
<param name="imagelist_0" value="egor1.gif, egor2.gif, egor3.gif,
egor4.gif, egor5.gif">
<param name="URL_0" value="http://www.bookcenter.com">
<param name="startpos_0" value="0,0">
<param name="move_0" value="0,0">
<param name="repeat_0" value="10">
<param name="timeout_0" value="5000">
<param name="bounce_0" value="true">
</applet>
```

You can change the Web page to suit your purposes or transfer the applet statement to another Web page. Matching the Web page background color to the background color of the applet presents a polished presentation.

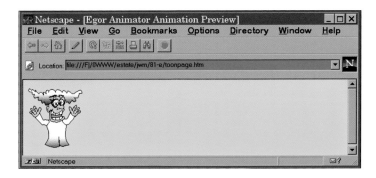

The key to using Egor easily and effectively is setting it up properly. Pay close attention to installation to ensure that the appropriate files are in the specified directories (folders). The preview feature under the Preview tab requires that you have the Java Software Development Kit (SDK, available at `http://www.javasoft.com`) set up on your hard disk. Alternatively, you can preview your Egor animation applets with your Web browser without the Java SDK.

You do not have to use the cartoon drawings that come with Egor. In the following animation sequence, a work of art materializes from a faded image.

By using the third image as the fifth image and the second image as the sixth image and then recycling, you can make the work of art fade in and out, as follows:

Sequence: 1 2 3 4 3 2 recycle

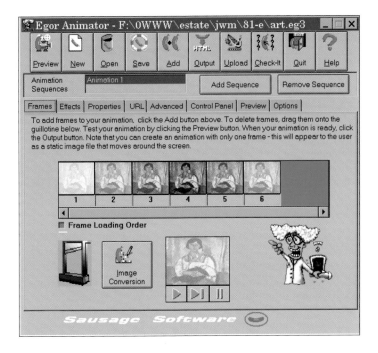

TIP If you can't draw and can't afford to hire an animation artist, try using Egor creatively with titles and headings that you create from fonts, or with images made from stock photos, stock art, or even clip art.

Egor also can make your animated graphic(s) move over the screen even as they are animating. Once you have mastered simple animation, explore using this advanced technique. ■

Jamba: Animated Graphic

Aimtech's Jamba is a well-endowed Java authoring program (Windows 95 and NT only). Although it is not yet enabled for general programming, it is a capable multimedia presentation maker, and its functionality expands with each new version.

Use Jamba as you would use a word processor. Instead of manipulating text, however, you manipulate a variety of media, including graphics and audio files. You will find Jamba similar to multimedia authoring programs, if you have used one (Aimtech of Nashua, New Hampshire (http://www.aimtech.com), developed Icon Author, a leading multimedia authoring program). The difference is that Jamba is a Java authoring program that you can use to create and compile a Java applet. Jamba also is useful for authoring applets that can deliver flexible multimedia capability to your Web site. A demonstration version is on the CD-ROM.

Although Jamba is not overly complex for nonprogrammers, it takes some time to learn it. It is best to start with a simple project before doing a more ambitious one. This section features the Aimtech Cool Logo demonstration project. You can see it on the CD-ROM, and it's a good project to start with. Use the demonstration on the CD-ROM together with this chapter to learn more about using Jamba.

NOTE **Because this is not a book specifically about Jamba, some of the default entries for the dialog boxes and some of the steps you will take to start authoring this applet may not be explicitly covered. However, Jamba has good software documentation. This section gives you the steps you need to create this applet after you have familiarized yourself with Jamba. A detailed step-by-step tutorial for learning to use Jamba is beyond the scope of the book.**

You begin with the StartPage object. This is the layout page that holds the text, graphics, and even icons for objects that represent other multimedia items such as audio bites. Make the layout area big enough to hold the graphic with a little room to spare. To make things easy on your eyes, you can change the background color immediately from white to green in the StartPage dialog box. Notice that the color settings are RGB, not hex.

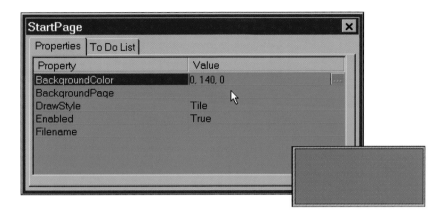

Next, add the ImageStrip object from the vertical row of objects on the left side by clicking on the object button and placing the white image object on the layout with the cursor. Right-click on the white object to bring up the object's dialog box.

The image (graphic) in this case is a series of images that will make up the animation (Coollogo.gif). As you can see, the images (cells) are in two columns and four rows for a total of eight.

177

TIP You must create the individual images (cells) or have a digital artist do it. Jamba comes with an image manipulation program, ImageLab, that you can use to easily make your image strip using the images you create. You also can use other programs that facilitate the creation of image strips.

Use the ImageStrip1 object's dialog box to set the characteristics for the graphic. For instance, enter the name of the graphic file Coollogo.gif.

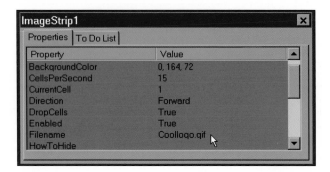

Next, enter information about the cell arrangement (in other words, 8 cells, 2 columns, 4 rows).

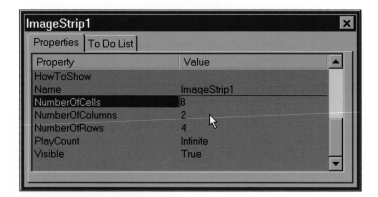

The graphic displays on the layout. Note that only one cell shows, not the entire graphic.

Next the applet plays an audio file. You add the audio using the Audio object. An icon representing the Audio object goes on the layout.

Set the characteristics of the audio presentation using the Audio dialog box. Note that one of the entries is the name of the audio file Coolsoun.au.

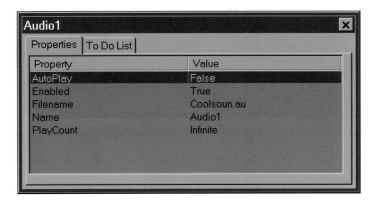

Next, go back to the ImageStrip1 dialog box and use the To Do List (in the dialog box) to set the method (action) for the image strip. Set Audio1 to Play() and ImageStrip1 to Play(). Consult the software documentation to choose a method appropriate for what you want to do.

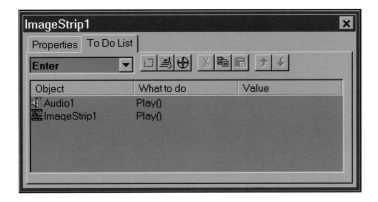

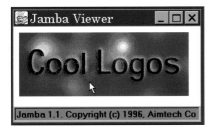

Now you're ready to test your new applet. Click the Run button on the toolbar.

This applet resides on a Web page. When a visitor to the Web site passes his or her cursor over the applet, it starts the audio and cycles through the cells giving an animated effect. Other than creating the art, you can make this applet in a matter of minutes once you have practiced using Jamba.

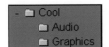

Jamba automatically creates a directory (folder) for your project with two to five subdirectories.

It's convenient to name the directory with the name of the project (coollogo, for example). Jamba creates and names the subdirectories Audio, Graphics, Text (ASCII text documents), Distrib (if needed), and Classes (if needed) and automatically places the requisite files in each directory. How's that for good management? Additionally, it places at least three files in the original directory: yourapplet.html, yourapplet.jmb, and yourapplet.jtf. The first file, yourapplet.html, is a Web page with the proper applet statement in it. You don't have to use this Web page, but it gives you the proper applet statement like the following for Cool Logo.

```
<applet codebase="" code="Aimtech.Player.class" width="300"
height="125">
<param name="fps" value="15">
<param name="filename" value="Cool.JTF">
<param name="page" value="StartPage">
</applet>
```

Notice that the codebase attribute stands ready to reference a remote Web site. You should delete it unless you intend to use it.

The second file, yourapplet.jmb, is the file you work with to create and revise the applet. You don't need this file to run your applet at your Web site server. You need it only on your own computer to revise your applet from within Jamba. The third file, yourapplet.jif, contains the instruction for the Jamba class files to run your applet and must be at your Web site server.

Jamba, with a built-in FTP client, automatically transfers all the requisite files, including the class files, via FTP to your Web site. After the requisite Jamba class files transfer to your Web site once, Jamba does not repeat the upload of such files when you revise and republish your applet. It simply transfers (uploads) the revised applet files.

TIP **Jamba places .zip files for Netscape Navigator in the applet directory. You use the** `archive` **attribute in the applet markup to reference a .zip file. Jamba also places the .cab files for Internet Explorer in the applet directory. The Jamba documentation provides the details for using the .cab files. See the "Getting Started" chapter for more information on .zip and .cab files.**

Jamba is a reasonably priced Java authoring program, sold at retail, which you can use to do much more than animate a logo. ■

Jamba: Multimedia Presentation

Jamba provides the capability to create complex applets that dress up your Web site with sound and graphics in action. (See the previous chapter for general information.) In this project, Jamba creates a self-starting presentation using three JPEG images, three arrow images (transparent GIFs), three text blocks, and five audio files (AUs). This is representative of a quick prototype presentation that you can create in a few minutes after you have some experience with Jamba. (Later you can come back and spend hours substituting dazzling graphics and fine-tuning the movement.) The first image and first text block appears in the upper-left-hand quadrant of a rectangular area. You can see this applet on the CD-ROM.

Next an arrow pointing to the right appears, followed by the second image and second text block in the upper-right-hand quadrant.

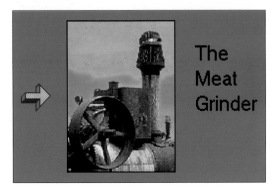

Another arrow follows, this time pointing down. The third image thereafter appears in the lower right-hand quadrant.

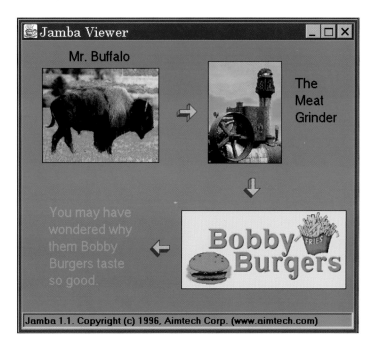

Finally, an arrow pointing to the left appears, followed by a block of text in the lower-left-hand quadrant.

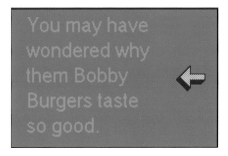

A sound accompanies each of these images—special sounds for each of the images and a click sound for the arrows. After this cycle concludes, it does not repeat itself, but you can easily program it to recycle, if you want.

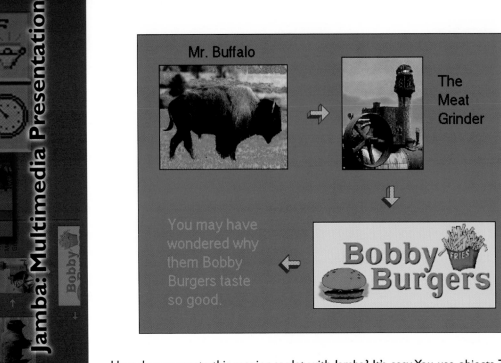

How do you create this moving applet with Jamba? It's easy. You use objects. The first object is the first image. The second object is the text block for the first image's heading. The third object is the audio file that accompanies the image. These objects combine to constitute the first event. The second event is the appearance of the arrow image (an object) together with an audio file (an object), and so on. In all, this applet contains seven events:

- JPEG, text, AU: first image with text heading and first sound
- GIF, AU: right arrow image and click sound
- JPEG, text, AU: second image with text heading and second sound
- GIF, AU: down arrow image and click sound
- JPEG, AU: third image with third sound
- GIF, AU: left arrow image and click sound
- Text, AU: text block and fourth sound

In this presentation each event consists of two or more objects, and each object represents a layer in the layout area. In addition, each event has a Timer object/layer that defines the event. Thus, the first event has four layers:

- Timer object
- JPEG object
- Text object
- AU object

Each succeeding event also has a Timer object/layer. The objects represent the Java programming. The layers represent the Jamba procedures that you use to author the presentation using the Jamba authoring program. The object/layers are the building blocks. Each object has its own capability and its own set of data, which you provide via the dialog box.

TIP As mentioned in the previous chapter, going through the authoring procedure from the beginning in great detail is beyond the scope of this book. You may find authoring to be detailed, often tedious work. One incorrect action or item of information can disable a substantial portion of an entire presentation. You must work with care and experiment a lot. You need about four hours of practice to create anything more than a simple applet such as **Cool Logo**. After such prolonged experimentation, you will work more quickly and efficiently. Jamba is not difficult; once you learn Jamba, you will be able to do what only Java programmers can do.

After opening Jamba, opening a new Jamba project, and starting a new page, you install an image object.

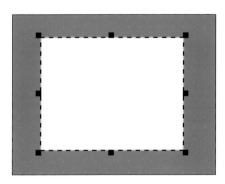

The Graphic1 dialog box enables you to define the image object.

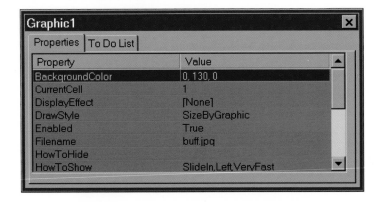

Next, install a text object.

Define the text object using the Text1 dialog box.

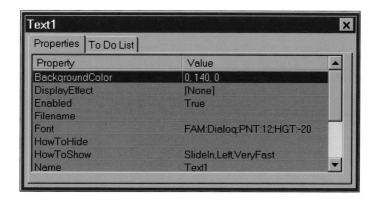

In this case, part of the definition is the text itself.

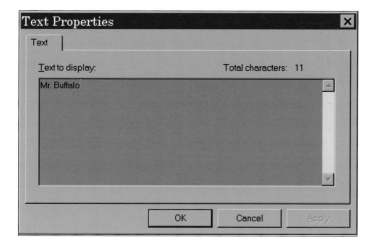

Next, install an audio object. Define it with the Audio1 dialog box.

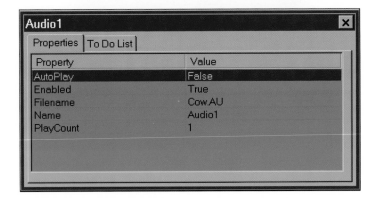

Now you're ready for the timer object. Define the timer with the Timer1 dialog box.

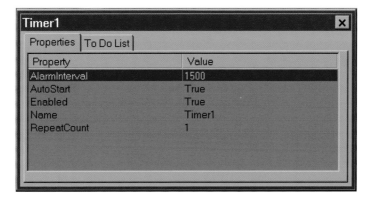

Because you want the timer to control the three multimedia objects you have installed, use the To Do List in the Timer1 dialog box and set the methods (actions) that activate the objects.

189

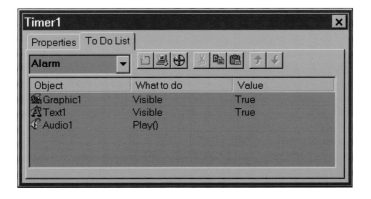

In this event, the graphic and text become visible (Visible originally set to False), and the sound plays (AutoPlay originally set to False). In this project, there are seven sequential events requiring seven timers. Every object used is associated with a timer object, which controls when each object materializes. The settings for the timer objects in milliseconds are:

- Timer1 object: 1,500 (1.5 seconds)
- Timer2 object: 4,000
- Timer3 object: 5,000
- Timer4 object: 12,000
- Timer5 object: 13,000
- Timer6 object: 21,000
- Timer7 object: 23,000

NOTE Logically you don't need a timer for the first event (Timer1), but it comes in handy to coordinate the first event with the second event.

In the first event, the graphic appears, the text appears, and the audio plays simultaneously. As you can see, this is a 23-second presentation, with each event happening in sequence. The project makes quite a menagerie of objects on the layout page.

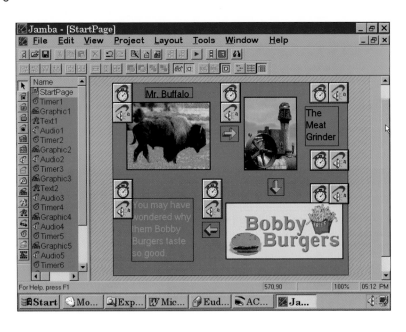

When the applet plays, however, all the icons representing the timer and audio objects disappear.

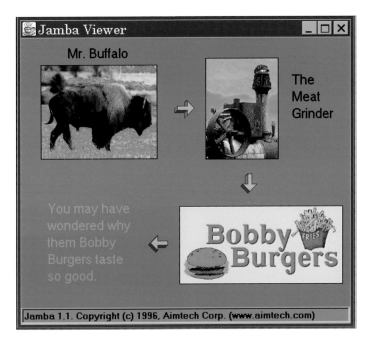

The layout area in Jamba is the same as the applet area on the Web page. The Jamba player—provided in Jamba to test your applets—shows only how the applet looks by itself and does not show the applet in a Web page.

This project is simple and straightforward. It makes a good self-training exercise because the timer object is difficult to learn. Jamba is capable of creating more complex presentations and programs than this, but this project gets you off to a good start as a capable Jamba user.

For information on how to publish your Jamba-made applet on your Web site, see the previous chapter. ■

Jamba: Moving Image

This applet made with Jamba makes a logo or other sprite image move across the screen horizontally from right to left. When it gets to the left side, it stops and a sound plays. This is a simple illustration of the power of Jamba to move a graphic anywhere on a Web page (within an area you define) in any direction at any speed.

The applet is a good learning device for creating well-timed and well-tuned animations. Other authoring tools may make creating this particular applet easier, but such tools don't provide the flexibility in movement and timing that Jamba does. Jamba can just as well enable wild movements over a large screen space or appearing and disappearing graphics combined with text. There are easier ways to do this applet with Jamba, but none are as instructional as this method.

The first part of this technique shows how you can use this applet on a Web page. The second part describes how you can create the applet in Java using Jamba. See this applet on the CD-ROM. (For more information on Jamba, see the "Jamba: Animated Graphic" chapter.)

The applet (gostrip) is a strip 450×52 pixels that does not occupy a large amount of screen area. It does accommodate simple substitutions. The graphic file image.jpg is 172×33 pixels. A graphic the same size will substitute well. A graphic with less width will not move exactly from the far-right side to the far-left side, but that will probably not affect the overall appearance. A graphic with a height greater than 52 pixels is partially obscured by the territorial limits of the applet.

A graphic file 450×52 pixels, back.jpg, provides the background. The audio file, sound.au, can be any size. Simply use the appropriate files you want to substitute (including GIFs) and rename them to image.jpg, back.jpg, or sound.au.

The applet makes a simple presentation. The image.jpg file travels from the far right to the far left.

A little improvisation can expand the applet's aesthetic effect. In this case, use the top.jpg and bottom.jpg graphics, each 172 pixels wide, to fit the image.jpg graphic. The image graphic moves across the screen to form a more complex logo with the top and bottom graphics on the left side. Not too fancy, but it will get your imagination stirring.

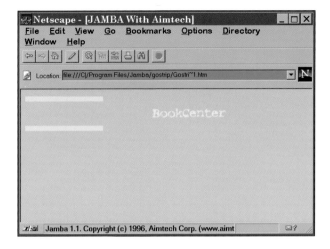

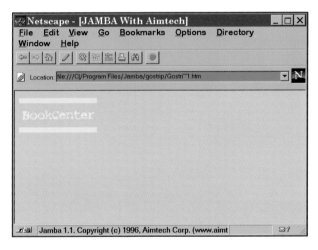

193

Do this by placing a graphic before the applet and one after the applet (top.jpg and bottom.jpg).

```
<img src="graphics/topbar.jpg" align="absbottom"><br>
<applet code="Aimtech.Player.class" width="450" height="52">
<param name="fps" value="15">
<param name="filename" value="gostrip.JTF">
<param name="page" value="StartPage">
</applet><br>
<img src="graphics/lowbar.jpg" align="top"><br>
```

There is nothing startling about this applet, but it can draw attention to a logo or image in an unobtrusive and dignified way—much like attractive letterhead stationery. Or, you can use it creatively for other purposes.

You start this applet in Jamba by setting the size.

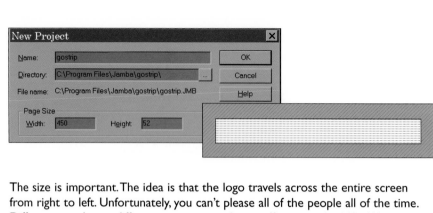

The size is important. The idea is that the logo travels across the entire screen from right to left. Unfortunately, you can't please all of the people all of the time. Different people use different monitor resolutions (for example, 640×480, 800×600, 1024×768). For a lowest common denominator, a width of 450 pixels provides a useful dimension for the 640×480 pixels resolution. For higher resolutions, a Webmaster can center the applet in the Web page. Using Jamba, you can change the applet to a greater width, if desired.

Setting the graphics for this applet is easy in Jamba. The initial graphic is the 450×52 pixels background graphic for StartPage.

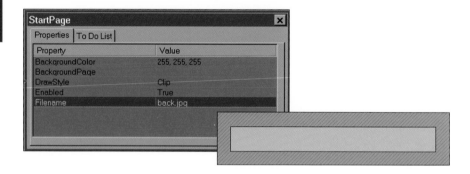

By making back.jpg, image.jpg, and the background color of the Web page the same color, you can create a seamless look. The other graphic is the logo or another sprite. Install it correctly the first time as Graphic1, and you can copy it easily for the remaining instances.

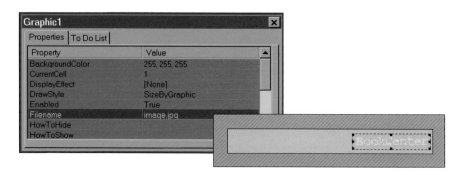

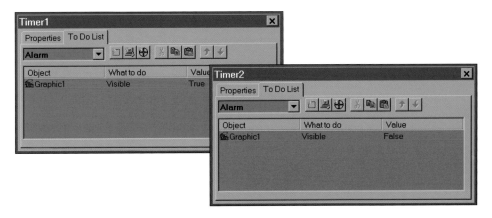

In this case, the image appears 25 times, each time a little farther to the left.

So, make sure that the first graphic object, Graphic1, is correctly set up before you copy it. Visibility, for instance, is set to False.

The key to making this applet work lies in using the time objects in Jamba. Two time objects are used for each instance of the graphic: one to change the Visibility to True (on) and a second to change the Visibility back to False (off).

Why two timers? You can use the same timer to change the Visibility of the displayed graphic to False and the Visibility of the next graphic to True, but using two timers provides greater control should you desire to make changes.

Changing the displayed graphic to False a few milliseconds before changing the next graphic to True may make the applet more stable as the graphic marches across the Web page. With timing, you always have to experiment and tune. Unfortunately, in this applet you end up with 49 timers instead of 25. Notice that you use only one timer for the final graphic because the graphic stays visible thereafter (Visible is True).

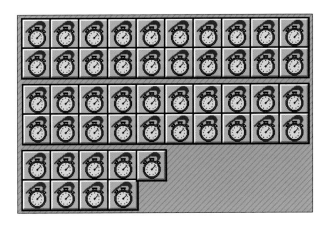

Again, the best way to create the timers is by copying one after another. Thus, it's important to set up the first one correctly. Unlike the graphic object, each of the timer objects has different data entries: Visibility (True or False), the AlarmInterval, and the specific graphic object affected. Other than that, each timer object is the same. So, copying makes sense.

Notice that the timers set an 11-second interval before the first graphic is displayed and another one-second interval before it starts to move across the Web page at an interval of one graphic per second. This seems to help stabilize the applet. In addition, the initial 12-second period provides flexibility if you want to create a preliminary presentation before the applet begins to move. If you want to make the applet wider, all you need to do is expand it (Project, Settings), reposition the existing graphics, and add more instances of the sprite graphic.

  TIP This applet is easy to create, use, and alter—but with one caveat: because the timing of the sprite graphic is difficult to tune, this Jamba project may take a lot of time to alter. Different computers play multimedia presentations differently. Just to get a sprite to move smoothly on one computer may require a lot of work.

Finally, add the sound with an audio object (Audio1).

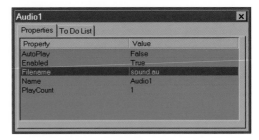

 The sound plays when the graphic gets to its final position (in other words, when Graphic25 appears).

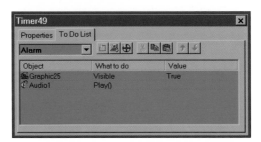

The applet is complete. Knowing how it works helps you change it in Jamba for your own use. ∎

Gallery

page 22

page 28

page 30

page 32

page 34

page 38

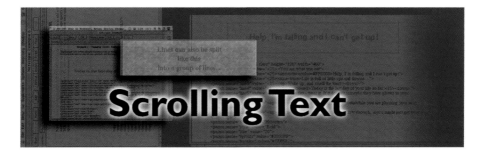

Slide Show

Fishing boats, Martinique

page 66

Rollover Button

page 70

page 76

page 80

page 94

page 98

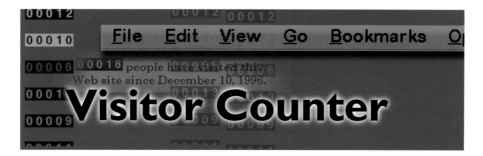

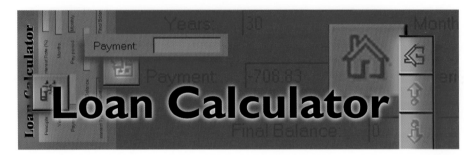

page 112

page 114

page 116

page 120

Spreadsheets

page 124

Office Applets

page 128

page 134

page 136

page 142

page 146

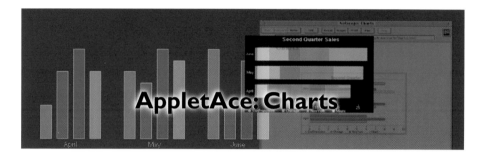

AppletAce: Charts

Riada Cartel: Running Marquee

Riada Cartel: Action Marquee

page 162

Egor: Animation

page 170

page 176

page 182

Jamba: Moving Image

page 192

Java™ Developer's Kit
Version 1.0.2
Binary Code License

This binary code license ("License") contains rights and restrictions associated with use of the accompanying software and documentation ("Software"). Read the License carefully before installing Software. By installing Software you agree to the terms and conditions of this License.

1. **Limited License Grant.** Sun grants to you ("Licensee") a non-exclusive, non-transferable limited license to use Software without fee. Licensee may re-distribute complete and unmodified Software to third parties provided that this License conspicuously appear with all copies of Software and that Licensee does not charge a fee for such re-distribution of Software.

2. **Java Platform Interface.** In the event that Licensee creates any Java-related API and distributes such API to others for applet or application development, Licensee must promptly publish an accurate specification for such API for free use by all developers of Java-based software. Licensee may not modify the Java Platform Interface ("JPI", identified as classes contained within the "java" package or any subpackages of the "java" package), by creating additional classes within the JPI or otherwise causing the addition to or modification of the classes in the JPI.

3. **Restrictions.** Software is confidential copyrighted information of Sun and title to all copies is retained by Sun and/or its licensors. Licensee shall not modify, decompile, disassemble, decrypt, extract, or otherwise reverse engineer Software. Software may not be leased, assigned, or sublicensed, in whole or in part. Software is not designed or intended for use in on-line control of aircraft, air traffic, aircraft navigation or aircraft communications; or in the design, construction, operation or maintenance of any nuclear facility. Licensee warrants that it will not use or redistribute the Software for such purposes.

4. **Trademarks and Logos.** Licensee acknowledges that Sun owns the Java trademark and all Java-related trademarks, logos and icons including the Coffee Cup and Duke ("Java Marks") and agrees to: (i) to comply with the Java Trademark Guidelines at http://java.com/trademarks.html; (ii) not do anything harmful to or inconsistent with Sun's rights in the Java Marks; and (iii) assist Sun in protecting those rights, including assigning to Sun any rights acquired by Licensee in any Java Mark.

5. **Disclaimer of Warranty.** Software is provided "AS IS," without a warranty of any kind. ALL EXPRESS OR IMPLIED REPRESENTATIONS AND WARRANTIES, INCLUDING ANY IMPLIED WARRANTY OF MERCHANTABILITY, FITNESS FOR A PARTICULAR PURPOSE OR NON-INFRINGEMENT, ARE HEREBY EXCLUDED.

6. **Limitation of Liability.** SUN AND ITS LICENSORS SHALL NOT BE LIABLE FOR ANY DAMAGES SUFFERED BY LICENSEE OR ANY THIRD PARTY AS A RESULT OF USING OR DISTRIBUTING SOFTWARE. IN NO EVENT WILL SUN OR ITS LICENSORS BE LIABLE FOR ANY LOST REVENUE, PROFIT OR DATA, OR FOR DIRECT, INDIRECT, SPECIAL, CONSEQUENTIAL, INCIDENTAL OR PUNITIVE DAMAGES, HOWEVER CAUSED AND REGARDLESS OF THE THEORY OF LIABILITY, ARISING OUT OF THE USE OF OR INABILITY TO USE SOFTWARE, EVEN IF SUN HAS BEEN ADVISED OF THE POSSIBILITY OF SUCH DAMAGES.

7. **Termination.** Licensee may terminate this License at any time by destroying all copies of Software. This License will terminate immediately without notice from Sun if Licensee fails to comply with any provision of this License. Upon such termination, Licensee must destroy all copies of Software.

8. **Export Regulation.** Software, including technical data, is subject to US export control laws, including the US Export Administration Act and its associated regulations, and may be subject to export or import regulations in other countries. Licensee agrees to comply strictly with all such regulations and acknowledges that it has the responsibility to obtain licenses to export, re-export, or import Software. Software may not be downloaded, or otherwise exported or re-exported (i) into, or to a national or resident of, Cuba, Iraq, Iran, North Korea, Libya, Sudan, Syria or any country to which the US has embargoed goods; or (ii) to anyone on the US Treasury Department's list of Specially Designated Nations or the US Commerce Department's Table of Denial Orders.

9. **Restricted Rights.** Use, duplication or disclosure by the United States government is subject to the restrictions as set forth in the Rights in Technical Data and Computer Software Clauses in DFARS 252.227-7013(c) (1) (ii) and FAR 52.227-19(c) (2) as applicable.

10. **Governing Law.** Any action related to this License will be governed by California law and controlling US federal law. No choice of law rules of any jurisdiction will apply.

11. **Severability.** If any of the above provisions are held to be in violation of applicable law, void, or unenforceable in any jurisdiction, then such provisions are herewith waived to the extent necessary for the License to be otherwise enforceable in such jurisdiction. However, if in Sun's opinion deletion of any provisions of the License by operation of this paragraph unreasonably compromises the rights or increase the liabilities of Sun or its licensors, Sun reserves the right to terminate the License and refund the fee paid by Licensee, if any, as Licensee's sole and exclusive remedy.

Java Web Magic

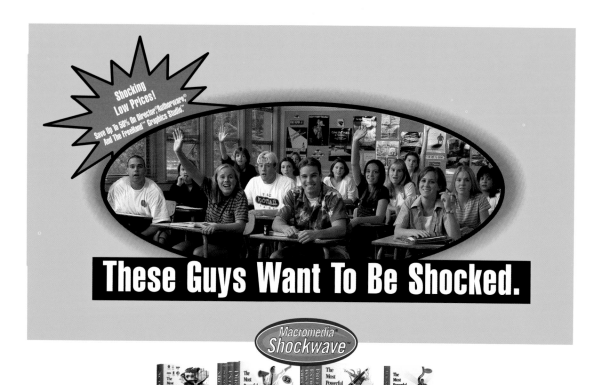

Here's Everything You Need To Do It.

Create and deliver electrifying education materials, from print to the Web.

Today's kids brag about baud rates. They work on new Pentiums or Power PCs instead of old Pontiacs. And they quote lines from Wired™ instead of Whitman.

Tough crowd.

But they're all yours if you have the Macromedia® Studios with Shockwave™. Products that help you create the hottest multimedia courseware and deliver it across campus or around the world.

You see, there's only one family of software for graphics and multimedia on the Internet. There's only one set of tools that helps you create everything from 2D to 3D to full-blown Web sites. There's only one name you need to know. Macromedia.

Take Authorware®, the educator's choice for interactive courseware and training— which now helps you create materials to be sent streaming across your intranet. Or the Director® Multimedia Studio,™ which sets the industry standard in multimedia. For illustration, page layout, font creation, hi-res image editing and 3D modeling, pick up the FreeHand™ Graphics Studio.™ And the Backstage™ Desktop Studio lets you create powerful database-driven Web sites, with no programming or scripting required.

To top it off, we're introducing electronic documentation versions of Director and the FreeHand Graphics Studio. Just another way Macromedia makes multimedia and graphics affordable for both educators AND students.

So here's your assignment: see for yourself how Macromedia can electrify your courseware and shock any audience. Call for our free brochure, "Macromedia in Education: 12 Case Studies," as well as the latest Showcase™ CD. Then take advantage of our new low education prices—just $649 for Authorware,®$249 for the FreeHand Graphics Studio,™ and $299 for Director.® And of course, don't miss our Web site.

The Macromedia Studios and Shockwave. Because when it comes to cutting-edge courseware, shock value is everything.

Call 1-800-220-5978
http://www.macromedia.com/

MACROMEDIA®
Tools To Power Your Ideas™

Java Web Magic

REGISTRATION CARD

Java Web Magic

Hayden Books

Name _____ Title _____

Company_____Type of business _____

Address _____

City/State/ZIP _____

Have you used these types of books before?   ☐ yes   ☐ no

If yes, which ones? _____

_____

How many computer books do you purchase each year?   ☐ 1–5   ☐ 6 or more

How did you learn about this book? _____

☐ recommended by a friend
☐ recommended by store personnel
☐ saw in catalog

☐ received ad in mail
☐ read book review
☐ saw on bookshelf

Where did you purchase this book? _____

Which applications do you currently use? _____

Which computer magazines do you subscribe to? _____

What trade shows do you attend? _____

Please number the top three factors which most influenced your decision for this book purchase.

☐ cover
☐ approach to content
☐ logo
☐ layout/design

☐ price
☐ author's reputation
☐ publisher's reputation
☐ other _____

Would you like to be placed on our preferred mailing list?   ☐ yes   ☐ no   e-mail address _____

☐ **I would like to see my name in print!** You may use my name and quote me in future Hayden products and promotions. My daytime phone number is: _____

Comments _____

_____

_____

Hayden Books   Attn: Product Marketing   ◆   201 West 103rd Street   ◆   Indianapolis, Indiana 46290   USA

Fax to **317-817-7440**   Visit out Web Page **http://WWW.MCP.com/hayden/**

Fold Here

BUSINESS REPLY MAIL

FIRST-CLASS MAIL PERMIT NO. 9918 INDIANAPOLIS IN

POSTAGE WILL BE PAID BY THE ADDRESSEE

HAYDEN BOOKS
Attn: Product Marketing
201 W 103RD ST
INDIANAPOLIS IN 46290-9058

MACMILLAN COMPUTER PUBLISHING USA

A VIACOM COMPANY

Technical
Support:

If you need assistance with the information in this book or with a CD/Disk accompanying the book, please access the Knowledge Base on our Web site at **http://www.superlibrary.com/general/support**. Our most Frequently Asked Questions are answered there. If you do not find the answer to your questions on our Web site, you may contact Macmillan Technical Support **(317) 581-3833** or e-mail us at **support@mcp.com**.

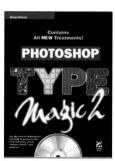

The *Java Web Magic* CD-ROM

The CD-ROM contains everything you need to bring the magic of Java to your Web pages—without programming!

- **Almost 40 Java applets** ready to cut-and-paste into your Web pages! You get all the class files associated with each applet, plus tutorials in the book for using them effectively.

- **Example Web pages** showing the applets in action.

- **AppletAce**—Macromedia's easy-to-use tool (Mac and Windows) for creating Java banners, bullets, imagemaps, and charts.

- **Jamba**—a PC Java authoring program ideal for multimedia presentations.

- **Riada Cartel**—a PC Java authoring tool that takes you through the process of easily creating applets.

- **HTML Editor**—a Macintosh HTML program.

- **HTML Assistant Pro 97**—a PC HTML program that includes a color picker.

- **Mapedit**—an imagemap creation tool for the PC.

- **HTML ColorPicker**—the easiest way to convert color values on a Mac.

- **Sound Hack**—a cool shareware sound editor for the Mac.

- **GoldWave**—a PC audio editor.

- **GraphicConverter**—the ultimate file format converter for the Mac.

- **Demo versions** of Macromedia Backstage Designer, SoundEdit #16 , Extreme 3D, and more.

- **And even more useful tools!**

 NOTE **Some of the software included on this CD-ROM is provided as shareware for your evaluation. If you try this software and find it useful, you are requested to register it as discussed in its documentation.**